# *Stoneg*
# *Voices*

*Van Wilson*

Published by York Archaeological Trust 2009
47 Aldwark, York YO1 7BX
www.yorkarchaeology.co.uk

Designed and typeset by Lesley Collett, York Archaeological Trust
Cover design by Lesley Collett

Printed by Sessions of York

ISBN No. 978-1-874454-44-1

*Front cover: (top) Stonegate in 1908-1910 (by permission of Mulberry Hall);
(bottom) Stonegate in 2009 (Lesley Collett)*
*Back cover: Stonegate c. 1909 by Val Prince*

# CONTENTS

## Foreword

The reminiscences contained within this book, from some 70 men and women who lived or worked in the central Stonegate/Swinegate area of York, together with detailed research and some excellent photographs, paint a wonderful and evocative picture of life in the area from the 1920s.

The area nowadays is a tourist haunt, boasting elegant shops, restaurants and bars, but when I was growing up in York it was home to craftsmen, local businesses, small shops and warehouses. I'm thrilled to see my father, GP Dr Reginald Dench, who had a practice here, referred to by several interviewees, and also my mother, Olave Dench, who used to attend St Helen's Church.

I would like to wish York Archaeological Trust every success with this book which allows local people to record their experiences and so add their own stories to the history of the fine city of York.

*Judi Dench*

## Chapter 1

# Coffee Yard and Barley Hall

*Coffee Yard before 1893. The exposed medieval roof timbers and trusses can be seen.*
*(Image reproduced courtesy of City of York Council, Local Studies Collection)*

Coffee Yard in the late 19th century was a fairly derelict area. Betty Powell was born at number 4 in 1930 at her grandfather John Nelson's two-up two-down house, and recalls that it was quiet and rather dark. There were only two houses occupied at that time, numbers 1 and 4, with Woodhouse, the wood turner, the North Radio Supply Company and the York Tyre and Vulcanising Service based in the rest of the yard. By the end of the decade, there was only one residence, and Auton's plumbers had moved in, alongside Jackson's Signs.

1

Kathy Parker's father, Jeffery Ledward, worked for Jackson's Signs from the early 1950s.

*Then he bought the firm in 1957. It was started by a Mr Jackson in about 1934 and he did have a shop in Stonegate itself as well as work-shops in Coffee Yard.*

*Going from Stonegate into Coffee Yard, it would be on the left and the passageway went underneath Auton's plumbers' workshops. It was L shaped, we were in the long bit. In the shorter bit were Noel Wain-house electricians.*

NOEL WAINHOUSE

ELECTRICAL ENGINEER
REPAIRS & INSTALLATION
ADVICE & ESTIMATES FRLI
Phone: DAY. YORK 54268 & NIGHT. YORK 59840
COFFEE YARD,
STONEGATE, YORK.

*The front workshop, they called it a lean-to which I found very insulting because it was very solid, it had a flagstone floor. An American gentleman came to see us in the '70s, who had traced his family back to York. He found that, with the river being tidal at York, there were shipbuilding firms along King's Staith and they would take wood from the ships and use them in buildings. He maintained that the main, great big square piece of wood that went up right through the building, was from a big Spanish type galleon. Nina and the Pinto came to York so I understand, ones that went with the Santa Maria. The place felt very medieval. The staircase to the upper workshop was just like a big wide ladder.*

*I can't ever remember a time when I didn't go there. My mum would come and do the book keeping every Thursday and I'd be on her bicycle on the little seat. When Dad bought the business, we got a Ford van with it. I spent a lot of time as a child playing with putty and blowlamps and shellac and paint, and as much paper as I could write on. Generally making a mess but keeping amused.*

*I started to occasionally help him properly, my first job went out when I was eight years old. I'd painted the background. During holidays I was probably more with him than I was at home. He would write vehicles on the premises where they were. He was often there at 11 o'clock at night just to get another coat on. The thing that really*

*affected us was pedestrianisation, because it was very difficult to get deliveries in and for customers to come and pick up. They weren't just a roll of posters, it would be a great big sign. We'd park in Swinegate but it was still running the gamut with parking attendants. We had a Labrador and he once went down there to put another coat of paint on, and when he came out there was a parking warden putting a ticket on. He said, "I've just unloaded some stuff". "You haven't, you've been taking your dog for a walk".*

*Monday mornings were awful because people had staggered through the yard from the Starre Inn and there was vomit and broken glass and all kinds of things to clear up. About twice a year my dad would*

3

get called out on Saturday night by the fire brigade or police to say somebody had set alight to something. One night there'd been a fire and the place was just ankle deep in water.

We had all sorts of customers. Anybody who needed advertising, estate agents particularly, and auctioneers and valuers. Right on the corner of Stonegate and Coffee Yard was Ben Rider's estate agents. And Dowsett Engineering, we did all their vehicles. I've known my dad be ill and sitting out in the street on South Bank Avenue in his dressing gown and a towel round his neck, writing a Land Rover while it was still running. He'd often do vehicles if they'd been spray painted somewhere or some finish put on them. There was a lot of poster writing for shops. One of the first deliveries I ever did was to Iles in Parliament Street that sold gloves, hats and handbags. And it would be 'Half Price Sale'. They did the most marvellous Christmas displays. They had a wonderful igloo all made out of card and painted and all glittering. They'd have little motors behind them so the wings moved. He loved doing anything like that.

We had a hand cart if you were working in town. It would be loaded up with paint. He would gild big windows, and write on shop windows. But one of the big poster things would be the York Festival every four years. I remember when I was about twelve, we had to go round every morning before 8 o'clock, there were four great big boards, one was in Duncombe Place and one was near Clifford's Tower and before I went to school, we pasted posters on top of the old ones. But he never taught me to write. He didn't have time to. He could do it quickly himself. I second coated, I could go up to the edges but I didn't do anything freehand.

One thing that became popular in the '70s, pubs like the Half Moon in Blake Street became a themed pub. It was all pirates, the signs were pieces of wood with bits missing, and Dad had done it all out. The shop fitter asked if we would go and do a job in Manchester 'cos he had *a big pub there to do. They were changing it into a fairground pub and the bar was like a carousel. I was 15 and it was the summer holidays and I went with my dad and we boarded there. This guy said, "You can bring your daughter, but I will not be responsible, she will hear all sorts of language, I'm not going to tell my blokes to quieten it down". It was very rough and ready, but it was very interesting. So he did do jobs away every now and then, he did a lot for power stations.*

*We used to get paint from Bellerby's in Grape Lane. They sold paint and wallpaper. My dad did work for them just after the war and they worked in the Minster gilding choir stalls. We had a blacksmith that did our work as well. He eventually had a place on Foss Islands Road, a forge there, he would make all the fittings and the brackets. Another part of my dad's job was to apply for planning permission so he would have proper scaled drawings and illustrations. Architects were not held in great esteem by signwriters because their plans weren't precise enough. We were asked to go somewhere in Scarborough and put a For Sale sign up but they hadn't highlighted the property on the plans. We wondered why we had to climb over the fence. He'd picked me up after school and I'd gone with him and next morning we found we'd actually put the council depot up for sale. So we had to go back and take it down. All these honours boards, they're all done in gold. A lot of golf clubs used to like him to go, and public schools. He did a lot at Howsham Hall.*

*At the bottom of Coffee Yard was that little cottage which is now part of Wilde's. That was Mrs Deamer's and her son Raymond was a photographer in Stonegate. I remember my first passport pictures were taken by him. It seemed like a tiny house but it goes a long way back. Then there was the Yorkshire Wholesale Fruiterer in Swinegate. We never had a bag of apples, my dad always bought a box at the beginning of the season. And Hannon's, I remember the first time he brought an avocado pear. I remember him coming back with stuff. "This has been flown in from Israel". You felt as if they'd been dropped by parachute into Stonegate.*

5

*Swinegate, c.1934 From a newspaper article , York Citizen, January 1994*

*We often used the actual yard to work in. My dad called it Number
4 workshop. People would come through and they'd be trying to read
the signs. On purpose he'd write an E out of the second word and an
I out of the first word. It's almost like Rolf Harris, "Can you tell what
it says yet?" Before I was born they'd had a couple of motorcycles in
the yard that were used for jobs. I know one apprentice was revving
a motorbike up, facing towards the stairs that went up into Auton's,
and he slipped it into gear by accident and shot up those stairs. They
had a lot of fun in there as well. It was so warm when the sun was out
in summer, you could feel it baking as it got closer. We'd get peacocks
from the Museum Gardens up on the roof and they'd be sitting
squawking. We were more or less level with them upstairs in the workshop. It was certainly an interesting area. I went to Doncaster and
came back to York in 1974, and helped my dad out in the evenings.
Knowing the place from being tiny, I never had any worries about*

being there on my own, but the dog sometimes, she'd suddenly stare at a spot and start to growl. Then you start to think about how old it was, what had gone on in this building. I think the York Courant had a workshop there. Lots of walls were covered in that plaster and horse hair, and there were huge holes in the floor in the poster shop.

We did quite a lot of work for Mulberry Hall. The Spode rooms upstairs, gilded on to the walls, that was real gold, it wasn't just gold paint. Then there was a café that became part of Mulberry Hall, the Coq d'Or. My mum and dad went to see Johnny Dankworth and Cleo Laine there during the festival, when they were dotted around at different venues. In my mind I imagined it being really avant garde.

We had one apprentice who tells all sorts of stories about working with my dad. The Hong Kong restaurant in Stonegate wanted them to do a job on a weekend so they didn't have to shut. On the Saturday night, my dad and Bobby and another guy were working in the base-ment, and they had red paint. Bobby tripped and spilt this paint all over himself. He came up out of the basement and absolutely terrified the poor waiters, they thought that it was blood. Then another lad came for a job. Dad was decorating this lady's house so he'd left him scraping down the wall to whitewash. My dad went to pick him up and found him laid out on this lady's settee with a cup of tea, and a cigarette. "What the hell are you doing?" "Oh don't shout at him, Mr Ledward, he's had an awful shock". Apparently he'd been up the ladder and fallen off, and was hanging through the roof of the toilet. This was only about his second or third day. Next day he put him on another job. He'd only been there 20 minutes and my dad got a call, "Would you come and pick him up and take him to hospital? He's trodden on a piece of wood with a nail in". But apprentices were always getting in trouble. One lad who eventually went to be a jockey, he was only the height of ten pennorth of copper. My dad sent him off with the handcart and he hit the kerb and I think it was Iles window in Parliament Street. Next thing dad's got a call, "Can you come and *remove your man?" He'd hit the kerb with this thing, all the paint shot forward and the window was like a rainbow, all different colours.*

*My dad was marbling some pillars at Hazelwood Castle, in the ballroom, it was green marble. When you're doing jobs like that, you have a ten gallon tin. This lad stepped backwards and tipped it up onto the ballroom floor. That all had to be cleaned up, so all the profits were taken up with my dad and a lad with wire wool scraping the floor. There were plenty of escapades. Another time, with his little Honda 50, Dad used to put all sorts on the back of it, and forgot he'd got a great big sign on it one day, and tried to get between two cars!*

Anne Nottingham recalls being

*A Guide in Coffee Yard in about 1932, the meeting place was in the upper room for the 43rd St Wilfrid's Guide Company. The Lieutenant was Cecelia Anthony, there were two patrols, Scarlet Pimpernel and Primrose. My friends were Winifred and Hilda Milburn, their grandfather was George Milburn, the sculptor who carved the monument of George Leeman. (See image on p. 31)*

David Harrison moved to Coffee Yard in 1971.

*The building was in a fairly run down state, as much of the centre of York was. There was a charity shop run by Minds Matter, it was the first charity shop in York. It was a bit shabby but people did come and use it. I know two people in York who are now near retirement who were students living there in the early '60s. There had been a plan at one time to pull it down and build a modern building, but fortunately that didn't take place.*

*One used to meet Stonegate traders, there was a Stonegate Day which was a service in St Helen's followed by a party in the Mansion House. The people have changed over so much and I get the impression they don't know each other in the way they used to. I think Alan Hitchcock had quite a lot to do with putting it together. He had the art gallery in the alley that leads down to the St Michael le Belfrey church hall.*

*I believe Tempest Anderson owned part of Stonegate from the Medical Society to the corner, which was in the 18th century owned by a York carpenter who carved quite a few things in the room upstairs. He let it off and the corner was*

*David Harrison, 2009 (Christine Kyriacou)*

*a pub the Saracen's Head. My cellar had Victorian tiles on the floor. A friend of mine said he could do a dig and we got down to Roman stone, and we found broken medieval pots, from about the 12th or 13th century. And a lot of animal bones and oyster shells in medieval oyster skin. I assume it was the kitchen quarters of a monastic dwelling before the goldsmiths took over.*

*The area around Swinegate was still called Benet's Rents. In the Middle Ages there'd been a church of St Benedict, Benet is a contraction of it, and it was pulled down in the Reformation. There were people who were carriers of sedan chairs. Two or three of them lived in Coffee Yard in the 18th century.*

*I remember after the 'snickleways' were set up by Mark Jones, [who wrote the book on The Snickleways of York] he gave a celebration in the 1980s called 'Handel in the Snickleways'. And he had Handel concerts, using a miniature organ. He did have dozens of people coming in to listen to Handel. I got a record player with stereo, in the*

9

*days of big records, the 33s, [long playing records], and I used to open my windows and play them rather loudly and I got rather well known for it.*

Peter Addyman was born in Harrogate in 1939 and came to York in 1972, although he knew the city quite well by then.

*Stonegate being one of the tourist spots in York, I must have gone up and down with Mum on occasion and subsequently I developed an interest in archaeology as a schoolboy, and one of the places you could go to do digs, of course, was York. George Wilmot was curator of the York-shire Museum and he was digging in the Abbey of St Mary's and around the Multangular Tower, so I came over when-ever I could and worked in the laboratory and in the museum.*

Peter Addyman
*(York Archaeological Trust)*

*I went off on to Cambridge and read archaeology and then became a lecturer in various universities. And in the early 1970s, York was undergoing a lot of development, and they were looking for an archaeologist. And Shelley [Peter's wife] and I decided it would be a more interesting life digging up places like York. So I came to set up York Archaeological Trust which has been carrying out digs all over the place including one or two in Stonegate. Every time anybody digs a hole, we've been there ready to look in it and so I'm possibly the person that knows more about what's underground in Stonegate than anybody else around now, having been looking at it from an archaeological point of view for a good 35 years.*

*The cellars in Stonegate go under the street, and when you see an* enormous lorry going up there, you shudder because you know it's hollow underneath in places. But those are fairly normal in any medieval town. One or two of our digs located an underground sewer of the Roman period. It actually starts off in Church Street and heads off in the Stonegate direction. And there's another one under York Minster that's heading off in the direction of Stonegate, quite a substantial tunnel made of great blocks of granite.

Stonegate runs along the line of the Via Praetoria of the Roman legionary fortress. It was the stone paved street that had been paved since the Roman period and in the Dark Ages and the Viking Age when it got its name, it was the 'stone street', running up the centre of the ancient city. On the north-west side of Stonegate we carried out quite a large dig in the mid 1970s, prior to the development

*Peter Addyman in the Roman sewer beneath Church Street, 1972 (York Archaeological Trust)*

of the arcade of shops. We excavated right down to Roman levels and found some of a crossroad of the Roman fortress, nicely cobbled, with very early period barrack buildings, way back into the first century AD. A little bit later than that, it was reconstructed like any Roman legionary fortress, the officers' houses, tribunes' houses, and we found part of a kitchen, one of the more impressive rooms of one of the Roman's tribunes of the legion. And in that area of the central part of

11

*Stonegate if you dug down about five or six metres, you should find more of these tribunes' houses.*

*There are other remains, the so-called Norman house which is still partly surviving in Stonegate because its walls had been left. The richer people or the owners would perhaps live in the Great Hall off the street front, and all the business-end of activity took place on the street front itself. And essentially that pattern is still there today.*

*The Norman House (Lesley Collett)*

*Barley Hall is an interesting story. It stems from the work that the Trust has done over the last 30 or 40 years on medieval sites around York. You dig up the remains of people's houses, and the alleys in which they lived, the yards and rubbish pits, so we know a huge amount about life in medieval York. You can come and marvel at wonderful churches and the Minster and fantastic glass and guildhalls but there was really nowhere that you can get a full feeling of what it was like to be an ordinary person in York. I'd always felt that what we needed in York was an ordinary house that you could go into, so that tourists can enjoy what we know. We had a similar feeling about the Viking Age, and we hit on the idea of what is the Jorvik Viking Centre, showing Viking life in York in a way that people could understand. So in the 1980s we had this bright idea of showing a medieval house and an ordinary citizen's life.*

*It needn't have been in Stonegate, but as it happened we were called in one day by Richard Wood, a well-known entrepreneur. His father was a famous Lord Mayor, Jack Wood, and the family has been running chemist shops for generations. Richard acquired this old building in Coffee Yard. He got some architects in to convert it into what were described as 'prestige offices'. And when we were asked to go in to do some archaeological excavation, I suddenly tumbled to the fact that actually there was more to the building than met the eye. There was most of a large medieval building in there, behind the plaster you could see the shape of the timbers, and it was right in the middle of the tourist zone, and actually fitted the bill for the idea of having a medieval house you could go into.*

*Eric Auton and his brother had owned the property, and Eric used half of it as a plumber's workshop. It was really the piece that is now the Great Hall and they worked on the ground floor and had an office upstairs and there was an internal stair, very different from what it*

---

Telephone **3074.**                                    Estimates Free.

FOR
# PLUMBING REPAIRS

CONSULT
# C. J. AUTON

BATHROOMS FITTED OUT              ■           **PLUMBER**
IN LATEST STYLES.                         SANITARY, HOT & COLD
REPAIRS PROMPTLY ATTENDED TO.                  WATER ENGINEER

*Address :*
## COFFEE YARD, STONEGATE, YORK

---

*looks like today, all sub-divided into smallish spaces. But it was quite good from his point of view because it was right in the middle of York where an awful lot of his work took place. And he was typical of many craftsmen and traders who worked in the Stonegate area before pedestrianisation.*

*We managed to persuade Richard Wood very kindly to sell 2 Coffee Yard to the Trust simply for what he paid for it. He was very proud of his York ancestry and loved the city and loved its history and, I think, almost in memory of his father, who as Lord Mayor had been for a year President of the York Archaeological Trust, he let us do this.*

*So there we were, with this crumbling old heap of all sorts of periods of construction from 20th century breeze blocks way back to medieval*

*David Black, RCHM, Professor Philip Dixon, University of Nottingham, architect Russell Wright and Maurice Barley, Chairman of York Archaeological Trust, at Barley Hall.*
(Peter Addyman)

*Reconstructing the roof of Barley Hall.* (Peter Addyman)

*timber work, with all sorts of alterations along the way. And the Trust set about the business of turning it into as near as possible a version of what had been there in the Middle Ages. It became quite a controversial project because normally when you're conserving ancient buildings you conserve them as found. Maybe there's some medieval timber work in it but there might be a Tudor fireplace and a 17th century sub-division and a 19th century fireplace and plastering, a story of the life of the building through hundreds of years. We felt that the whole purpose of this exercise was to show a medieval building. I wouldn't normally do this but for this particular purpose, and just this once, I felt that it was worthwhile sacrificing some later stuff, to get back to what was a very interesting early medieval building.*

*First of all we had to raise money to do it, and secondly we had to find an architect who was sympathetic. We were extremely lucky, because*

15

*Richard had already identified Russell Wright, a conservation architect. He was very much attuned to York and he'd done his dissertation on Coffee Yard!*

*The question then was, how on earth do you restore a medieval building to as near as possible its original state when some bits are missing? And the techniques you are going to be using have to be medieval ones. We identified somebody who was up and coming in the business of restoring timber-framed buildings, a wonderful chap called Peter McCurdy, and he had a farm with huge 16th century barns at Stanford Dingley, and he was helping restore other buildings around the country. And we decided the technique was to restore all the bits that were reasonably fully there, but the ones that required a lot of work we'd simply take down, ship down to Stanford Dingley, re-build in his great 16th century barns and bring them back.*

*So it was a heroic performance. Coffee Yard is off Stonegate, right in the middle of the tourist area and everything is tightly packed and built up. How on earth do you do a big construction job in the middle of all that? And the answer is you do it in the middle of the night. We were able to take the huge timbers down over a period of weeks, and then bring back the restored and even larger timbers and shunt them through in the middle of the night.*

*We had a wonderful chap, Charles Kightly, a historian particularly interested in medieval social history, who had done work on the documentary sources for our building. It had been owned by Nostell Priory, and in the Middle Ages the Prebend of Bramham was the Prior of Nostell. And its documentary history is quite well-preserved. They put up a hospice there, which was a place they could come to and stay in when they were having business in York.*

*Some of that hospice is still there, it's the north-east wing of Barley Hall. The priory was in need of money in the 15th century and added*

*Exterior of the reconstructed Hall. (York Archaeological Trust)*

*a Great Hall to it, and then let it out as a sort of commercial let. A
number of worthy local York citizens were tenants. Charles Kightly
identified one of them as a well-known medieval character called
William Snawsell. He was Lord Mayor of York, on the City Council,
a goldsmith. He's there in the minutes of the council. And there is
an inventory for a goldsmith's house in Stonegate at the right time.
So it's been furnished and decorated in a way that is pretty accurate,
based on what we know from those inventories, because they often talk
about the wall-hangings and furniture. Now you can step back into
the past, and get the feel for what it was like to be a fairly rich local
businessman in the late 15th century.*

*So how do you furnish a medieval house when there's no medieval furni-
ture down at Habitat? You have to decide what would be appropriate. So
for example we have a settle copied from one in the Victoria and Albert*

17

*Museum. We knew that William Snawsell had a large oak chest. His granny's will left him 'my old red Flemish chest'. And so we found one in the church at Wath near Ripon. So we replicated that and the chest in the steward's room in Barley Hall is based on that one.*

*We had objects that fitted the bill, and there was quite lot of pottery and stuff from the site. We got hold of a marvellous chap called John Hudson who specialises in medieval and post-medieval pottery over at Mirfield. We had wills and inventories, and many manuscript illumi-nations of the 15th century that show what the floor was like and so you can reconstruct it. Using documentary sources about how people organised their lives, you can fill in the other details. 90% of what is in Barley Hall is based directly on some kind of evidence, archaeolog-ical, historical or illuminated manuscript.*

*Once you've started a project like that you've got to finish it. And there are always difficulties. One of the problems that I had was reconciling the needs of modern archaeology with the needs of a construction team. I was also the restraining influence so far as the archaeology was concerned. We caused Russell Wright huge amounts of heart-searching and pain by insisting that before any bit of earth was removed, it had to be excavated. And we had a team led by Kurt Hunter-Mann, a very clever archaeologist employed by the Trust, and a building recording group led by Martin Stockwell, a Trust field officer. I felt we really shouldn't be destroying this Victorian front room or this 17th century sub-division, and the only justification was having it properly recorded. And so there were times when the needs for recording and the needs for construction were in conflict.*

*It wasn't an easy job. We did it in close association with the City of York's historic buildings people. We also had English Heritage breathing down our neck. We weren't treating it as a historic building in the traditional way, we were going to create something new. But there is an organisation called the Society for the Protection of Ancient*

*Buildings, or SPAB, and when they heard we were taking out post-medieval structure, they were not amused and complained bitterly. So not only do you have the architect not wanting the archaeology to be done, or the constructors wanted to get on before you'd managed to record the wall, and all these technical and practical problems, but you had SPAB breathing down your neck. I normally subscribe to SPAB and all its objectives but felt that just once it was worth trying to show what a medieval building might have been like. I wouldn't want to recommend it to be done generally. At times in the middle of the night I'd wake up and think, "You shouldn't be doing this Peter", but in the morning I would say, "No, it's a great project and we really must complete it". And the net result is a lovely place that has given huge joy to generations of visitors.*

*We needed to raise money and we needed a high profile person. At that time Robert Hardy was very well-known for his acting but was also engaged with the Mary Rose Project. He became very high profile on medieval archery. We showed him the project and he got deeply involved and agreed to essentially be the public face of Barley Hall. And we had various fund-raising events and he was a significant help. And also while we were building Barley Hall up, along came Sam Wanamaker, Zoë Wanamaker's father and a very famous film man, whose dream was to re-build the Globe Theatre. He came up several times.*

*One of the nicest stories about Barley Hall – I went over to lecture in Chester and two little old ladies came up and one of them said "I'm your cousin Helen, next time you come to Chester, come to dinner". So next time I lectured at Chester I took up her invitation. She was very charming and we got on very well and she said, "I really like Barley Hall, it's wonderful. I'd like to do something. Can I give you £50?" So I thought that was very nice. And I met her one other time, then one day I got a phone call from a solicitor in Liverpool who said, "Your cousin Helen has died". "Yes, I've heard that, it was very sad". He said, "I'm just dealing with her will and she's left the York*

*Robert Hardy in Thomas Gent's Coffee House* (Peter Addyman)

*Archaeological Trust £290,000." It was because she was so impressed by what we were doing and she so loved Barley Hall. And dear Helen is commemorated with a piece of furniture, called 'the English chair'. It's a painted chair of the middle of the 15th century, so that's Helen's chair.*

*When we developed Barley Hall as a place for visitors, I had a vision of an ideal museum set-up whereby you get people's attention, take them through and get them excited and then make sure they go through a souvenir shop and slake their thirst in a refreshment area. And there was a little area that was definitely not medieval, it was 18th century, a rather elegant little addition on Coffee Yard. It had several coffee shops in the 18th century. So Russell Wright did a beautiful replica of an 18th century coffee shop from an engraving. And it was full of wonderful feeling. It was candlelit and there was a cellar below and you went down and it really did feel like some 18th century dive. We decreed that you shouldn't sell anything that wasn't around in the 18th century so although we did sandwiches because the Earl of Sandwich just about got in under the wire, we couldn't do tomato sandwiches, because they thought tomatoes were poisonous in those days. We called it Thomas Gent's, the publisher who had a shop in Coffee Yard. He used to publish The York Courant from there.*

*It was lovely, a wonderful place you could take visitors and I do remember distinguished visitors. A lot came to see the project because York got a wonderful reputation for interpreting the past. I remember Mo Mowlam the Labour politician coming one day and we showed her round and she really laid down the whole of the future of the cultural development of museums around this coffee house. And we had a delegation from the parliamentary heritage group so there was a coffee shop full of MPs and distinguished politicos there at one stage. We even had the Queen of Norway having a cup of coffee. It was great but it never made a profit because we may be good archaeologists, but we're not terribly good at making profits out of sandwiches.*

*We acquired the building in Coffee Yard about 1986, but it wasn't until about 1990 that it was actually brought into its proper state, and I believe it opened in 1992. At that time the Trust's chairman was a very distinguished architectural historian called Maurice Barley, Professor of Archaeology at the University of Nottingham. He was really important, because he was a national expert on timber-framed buildings of the Middle Ages, and he chaired an Advisory Committee as to how to bring this project through.*

*We thought it would be a tribute to the huge number of hours and vast number of miles that Maurice and [his wife] Diana had devoted to this project and to the York Archaeological Trust, to name it Barley Hall after Professor Maurice Barley. There is in the Great Hall a great arch-brace in the main truss, and right at the top where the arch comes to a point inside the hall there had been a carved wooden boss like the bosses in the roof in the Minster, but it had been chopped off. We thought when we were restoring that, "What shall we put on the boss?", and hit on the idea of a couple of barley corns and so they twine together up there, beautifully carved by a very talented young carver from the York Minster masons' workshop. Very sadly Maurice died before we completed the project, but his wife Diana came up and opened it, and we had a wonderful and very touching ceremony.*

*Barley Hall was an absolutely wonderful project, to go through every little detail of life in the Middle Ages and try and find some evidence for it and interpret it in a way that becomes a living museum, and people see all this unconsciously and take it in, because actually the very best archaeological and historical advice has been taken and it is the best guess we've got in the 21st century.*

*Interior of the reconstructed Hall (York Archaeological Trust)*

## Chapter 2

# *A Child's Eye View*

Today there are no residential properties in Swinegate and only a handful of people live in Stonegate, but a hundred years ago the area was well populated. Stonegate was always a fairly affluent area, and business people often lived above their premises, whereas in nearby Swinegate, Grape Lane, Little Stonegate and Coffee Yard, there was quite a contrast. In the last few decades of the 19th century, Swinegate was filled with lots of small craftsmen. There was a hatter, plasterer, toy dealer, clog maker, brewer, comb maker, coachmaker, tailor, baker,

*Swinegate c.1900. Grape Lane is on the left, Mad Alice Lane behind the group of children on the right. (Image reproduced courtesy of City of York Council, Local Studies Collection)*

provision dealer, fried fish dealer, ale and porter stores, music instrument maker, furniture dealer, whitesmith, glass blower, hay dealer
and even a cow keeper. The 1901 census lists 195 people living in
Stonegate.

Alethea Asplinn was born at 12 Little Stonegate in 1905.

*It was at the back of Coultas and Vollans the printers, and quite dark.
Father worked at the Minster for 22 years, taking visitors to the top.
It was a nice little house. We had a passage, sitting room and kitchen.
Then cellar steps outside to the toilet and washhouse. I was always
frightened to go down there. One day I found one of the girls from
Coultas and Vollans. She'd fainted on the seat, frightened me to death.
The girls used the toilet but not the men, they went round the corner.
We never had a bathroom there, just a big tin bath in front of the fire.
There was a big house next to the printing works, a bookie's, they were
a bit posh. Then the piano people had a store place. Kilvington's wire
shop on the corner had a workshop and they used to sing 'Come into
the garden Maude' to our Maude. At the back of Bullivant's butchers,
we'd draw a line and play French cricket. Or we would play hopscotch
or Iddy Eye Opey. I learnt to ride a bike round the Minster. There
wasn't much traffic, only the coalman. And a man with an organ and
monkey came round. I went to St Michael le Belfrey, was christened
and confirmed there. Sunday School on a morning was in the church
lane in Stonegate. I was seven when the Titanic went down. I can
remember singing 'For Those in Peril on the Sea'. At Christmas we
always had a stocking, an orange and a new penny. Dad would take
me to Victoria Hall [in Goodramgate], for a penny in the bucket on
Saturday afternoon. We saw silent films like Pearl White who would
lay across train tracks, it stopped at the exciting bit, Rin Tin Tin or
the Sheik of Araby.*

*In the First World War, most of the people from Little Stonegate used
to come down the steps when there was warnings on and my dad*

*took me up once and I saw a Zeppelin going over. They'd bombed St Saviourgate and a friend of mine had her arm injured. My two uncles had farms outside Ely and would send us stuff so at Christmas we always got duck or chicken. You couldn't get butter, so we had bread and dripping.*

*We had a piano at home. I learnt but my eldest sister, she was eight years older, played by ear. She played for wounded soldiers. We used to have them for tea in the First World War. They'd play whist, but I was only young and I had to go to bed.*

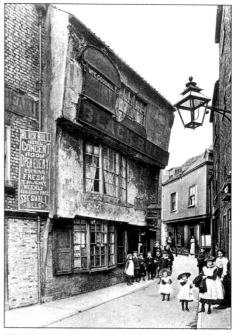

*The Black Bull public house, c. 1900*
(Hugh Murray)

*We moved to live in Coney Street but then back to Stonegate and lived above Bruce's fruit shop. You went down the passage of the Starre Inn to the front door. We stayed there till the year before I was married, we had lovely nights in Stonegate. Policemen walked round and tried every shop door. Once when I was courting, the policeman shone a light on us in the shop doorway and said, "Come on, let's have you out of here". I said, "I'm sorry I live here". We've come home from dances and a policeman would be sat in the chair. When my mother died, my dad never bothered with anyone else ever. Every night in Stonegate, I'd go to t'Starre for a gill of beer for him and he'd have his beer and bread and cheese for supper. When mother was alive, they went out to Benson's in Market Street on Saturday night. You could get a pie and a drink of beer. This was pre 1914.*

*At the end of the First World War, we had a street party in Little Stonegate. When t'fair was in the market, it used to be lovely. A cakewalk went up and down and you could dance. I've only seen it once since then. You went up Black Bull passage to the market [St Sampson's Square]. There was a slipper bath there as well. Old Mr Chaplin sold roast potatoes and you could buy fresh eggs and curd.*

Joan Sadler was born at 23 Swinegate in 1922,

*when Swinegate was a very, very built up area. We lived next door to Mr Lambert's garage. And you went up this short step and there were six families in this square. The rent for our house was 6/6d a week. It was only two up and two down. We shared a toilet and a yard with the people next door. We had a living room and a kitchen, and two bedrooms but it was tiny. We had a double bed up against the wall then a dressing table, [Joan and her twin sister]. The wardrobe was on the landing outside. We didn't have many clothes anyway. We never had any toys. Just snakes and ladders and tiddlywinks.*

Joan Sadler in the 1940s

(Joan Sadler)

*Where the Mulberry shop is, [junction of Swinegate and Grape Lane] that quite expensive shop, was the Coach and Horses, the man who had it was Robert Nutbrown. Over the Elim church was a billiard hall. The area was busy, with it being in the heart of the city. We were christened at St Sampson's and went to Sunday School there. I think there were three pubs in Church Street, and there was a slaughterhouse at the bottom of Patrick Pool. I used to go and run errands for a lady in Finkle Street. The first cut price shop was in Church Street, a long time before the war. These people came from Leeds.*

*The Elim church opposite us, seemed to be there as long as I can remember. And what was the café till recently, was a cycle shed for bank people from the Midland Bank in Parliament Street. We only knew one, a Mr Mason who lived in Claremont Terrace.*

*Sadd's in Goodramgate near Monk Bar, was a double fronted shop, and sold nothing but bananas. My mother used to send us on Saturday teatime when they were selling them cheap. We always had banana custard for tea on Sunday. I can remember Saturdays,*

*The Coach and Horses Inn, Swinegate* (Hugh Murray)

*and the butter market when people from the countryside would sell their wares. They came in on horses and traps. And every week we had a rabbit. My mother was amazing at skinning it. She could do it in a matter of two or three minutes. We had marvellous rabbit stew. Yorkshire pudding with rabbit gravy was lovely. Then we'd take the skins to Clancy's in St Andrewgate and you'd maybe get a penny or tuppence.*

*We never went away, except to Scarborough with Sunday School. Our Saturday treat in summer was a walk to Bishopthorpe to the Marcia pub along the riverside. My father liked a drink and there was a tea*

*Elim Sunday School outing to Filey, June 25 1947. (David Watson)*

*garden. Later we'd go to the YWCA and the baths, St George's. My mother loved the theatre. She used to take us to matinees or we'd go to the Electric cinema in Fossgate. I didn't know any other children that went to the theatre. We had a wireless in Swinegate. You'd take batteries to be charged next door to the garage. I remember father saying, "Switch that rubbish off". It was Henry Hall, we thought it was nice music.*

*They were moving people out of Swinegate to new estates in Water Lane. They cleared everybody off and market traders used it for ware-housing. Now it's been upgraded amazingly. Mr Lambert who owned our property, his wife had a house to let on Heslington Road. So we moved to there.*

Godfrey Fowkes stayed with his grandparents at 23 Stonegate in the 1920s. Eighty years later he recalls some of the people who made an impression on him, at the age of nine or ten.

*In those years there seemed to be much poverty in the city. Little Stonegate, Swinegate, St Andrewgate and Coffee Yard were occupied by families living in extremely poor circumstances. Grandmother Wright was an extraordinarily generous person, so I was frequently sent along to various poor dwellings, with gifts of groceries, cakes, or freshly baked bread. There used to be a family who lived where Barley Hall now stands. They were very poor. I'd go there quite often.*

*Elizabeth Wright (Grandmother Wright) on holiday in Scarborough in the 1920s. (Godfrey Fowkes)*

*Although so young I was shocked and depressed by the evidence of deep poverty. In St. Helen's Square little boys were selling newspapers, barefooted in winter, on the corner where the Yorkshire Penny*

29

*Bank was at the time. And you encountered soldiers from the war, very often badly disabled, selling matches.*

*But those early days living in Stonegate, were very happy days for me. I enjoyed playing with the local boys on the Minster steps and up on the bar walls. We'd play cowboys and Indians. I recall the sons of Sidebottom's Antiques in Low Petergate, Scott's Butchers, the daughter from Seale's Brush Shop, and young Ben Kilvington from the wireworkers shop. Life was full of interest for a youngster. Watching grandfather's attempts to coax the sound from his crystal radio set with primitive earphones. Later with his assembly of coils, condensers, and a big horn loudspeaker, how entranced we were, for these were the golden days of jazz and the emergence of the great London dance bands, which became popular. I remember listening absolutely entranced to a weekly series of lectures by Dr Gilbert Murray on ancient history.*

*Another local event was the Gala, in the grounds of Bootham Hospital during the summer. I was taken along by my grandmother and was spellbound by the crowd and the exciting events on display. It was here that I witnessed a balloon ascent for the first time. People in the street appeared to know each other and found time to converse. There were more eccentric characters about the town, like Burlington Bertie who'd wander round in tailcoats and spats, and a very old man, James Melrose, lived in St Sampson's Square. He would wander round in very old fashioned clothing.* [Melrose was Lord Mayor and one of York's 'grand old men', he died in 1929 at the age of 100].

*There was always a man who I think had been an officer in the army. He'd walk up to St Helen's Square, take up a position in front of the Mansion House and do a smart salute. Grandma Wright's uncle was George Milburn, the sculptor. He had a place near Bootham Bar. He was the one who did the statue of George Leeman near the station and he was quite a well known character in York.*

We were friendly with people in the Minster. I can recall the bell, Great Peter. I remember being taken up and allowed to stand beside it when it struck 12 noon, it was very impressive. My strongest memory is of lying in bed on Sunday morning listening to the Minster bells. I used to love the sound.

**Audrey Peace was born at 17 Finkle Street in 1927.**

*George W. Milburn, sculptor, whose works include the statues of George Leeman and William Etty in Exhibition Square.*

*(Godfrey Fowkes)*

*It's now Victor J's wine bar. It was known as Mucky Peg's Lane. Tales differed, one said there was a prostitute that lived down there but somebody said it was called Mucky Pigs' Lane because when drovers brought stuff from the cattle market, that's where they drove pigs through into Swinegate.*

*My mum and dad had lived there from about 1925 and we left in 1939. There was two cottages, ours and number 16. It was only one room downstairs, L-shaped bedroom and attic and we had a tiny yard at the back. But we were posh, we had a flush toilet. I had a sister. We had one bedroom and mum had a partition across. We were lucky, we had a gas fire upstairs and quite a big range downstairs. We got a family [over the road] from Tadcaster, called Hardys. Mrs Hardy used to turn the rope at one end and me mother at the other and we'd skip. A lot of us got together and played in St Sampson's Square, at*

31

*Finkle Street in 2009: Victor J's cafe bar on the right is where Audrey Peace once lived.* (Lesley Collett)

'relievo'. One side would take the other side on. We shopped in Church Street. People got paid on a Friday and shops stayed open later. Often when we had our Friday night bath, we hoped me mother would go shopping 'cos my dad was much more fun. She'd take a basket and do her shopping at the Maypole, Melia's, Meadow Dairy, or greengrocery off the market. My dad was a railway worker. We were lucky, he was never out of work.

I think it had more character then that it has now. In Swinegate we had a little shop called Miss Calvert's. She was the other side of the road from the Coach and Horses. It was only a tiny shop but she sold everything from shoe laces to fresh eggs. You didn't buy in bulk. She had a book for them that got things on tick. They'd go in, ask for three eggs and give a name. I was that curious, I went and did it and gave my mother's name. I did get a good hiding for that. My dad thought it was amusing but my mother didn't.

Then you got your Friday's penny. And you got a ha'porth of this and ha'porth of that. Sweets were mainly fourpence a quarter. You'd get a cone bag. Dolly mixtures were popular 'cos you got a lot in, or kali [sherbet].

*Parliament Street market, 1920s* (Paul Stabler)

*I went into the fever hospital when I was five. The ambulance was in
Swinegate so they had to walk the full length of Finkle Street, every-
body turned out. There was a couple of women at each side who said,
"You'll soon be better". My sister had been in a few weeks before.
There used to be a notice go up outside the Guildhall, about diphtheria
and scarlet fever to tell you how patients were.*

*I was sad to leave there. Our house was just off St Sampson's Square
and it was a call-in place for a cup of tea. My mam had quite a few
friends and there was often a knock on t'door, on Friday and Saturday
afternoon. We only had one room but I've seen it absolutely full and
everybody sat having a cup of tea. They'd come with their parcels and
plonk them down.*

33

*I used to like going in the Minster. Sometimes, when I was 9 or 10, I'd go to Evensong. The first time I went, Father Tom took me and another girl round once after Sunday School. He was priest of St Sampson's. After that, if I was ever bored, I used to think, "I'll have a walk round t'Minster". I've walked round it many a time on my own. When I became a grandmother, that was one of the first places I took them.*

*Or on Sundays my dad would say, "Are we off for a walk?" And we walked to Sutton on Forest. That's when I started my first garden because I found some primroses and we shouldn't have done it, but my dad dug them up for me, and put them in a tomato box on top of t'toilet in the back yard in Finkle Street. Then I found some plants after t'stalls had closed down in the market. And I said, "Do you think these'll grow, dad?" And he got another tomato box, and they were French marigolds. We had a kennel for our dog, Nell. And we had to get a cat 'cos we got mice from t'builder's yard. Nell always slept in t'back yard. The only time she came in was when she pupped. We got up one morning and found out she'd had a litter of puppies which was wonderful.*

*I remember the party for the Silver Jubilee of George V and Queen Mary. We had a photo taken in the yard at the end of Grape Lane. A family called Deamers lived in that house and the party was in that yard. At one end of Grape Lane, a lot lived in rooms. I suppose they're called apartments now. There was about four or five terraced houses, then another passage which had a dog's home. Boxing Day was gift day and you took your dog and the dog got a gift and you got a gift. So there was a queue a mile long.*

*When I was about nine, I would wander about in the market and often get myself a little job, like straightening jumpers for a Jewess near the Primrose Café in Parliament Street. Then there was a quack doctor and he'd sell everything for curing ills. I'd watch out for him coming. He'd give me a white envelope with red stuff in it, a compound, and he'd say, "Break this up and put it in a mixing bowl". Then he'd send*

*Coronation party, May 12th 1937. Flo Brown, front row, fourth from left, hands in front. Granny Cox, eighth from right, white apron, leaning sideways. (Malcolm Brown)*

*me to Melia's for a pound of castor sugar. I'd light this little stove and fill the kettle, 'cos there was a water butt in St Sampson's Square, and put it on the stove. I had to stir it till it was dissolved, then wait for it to cool, then fill the bottles, and stick labels on. It 'cured every ill under t'sun'. He had some stones and he'd say, "These are what people passed after taking this medicine". The stones were off the cockles and mussels stall! He'd always give me half a crown so I used to be rich.*

*After Gran died, my mum and dad, my sister and I would go to the Rialto on a Saturday night. I always say my mother was the first woman's libber. We came home from school one day and my mother was there with a clean pinny and best blouse and skirt. When my dad got back from work, we were spruced up with clean ribbons in and my dad said, "Where are you off?" She says, "I'm off to t'pictures and I'm taking t'bairns with me. If you want to come you can come, but if you think I'm sitting in this house night after night, you've another think coming". And from then on we went to t'pictures every Tuesday and every Saturday night. My mam and dad had a happy marriage and we were a pretty happy household. You did make your own entertainment. I was quite good at dominoes and snap and my dad played tipitt with us. I remember Rhodes Brown's. I'd go in and was fascinated, 'cos the cash place was in the centre of the room and they put money in a little box and pulled a handle and it went off overhead. Then they'd take the money out and put a receipt back in and send it back again. I don't think shops can have the same fascination for children as they did for us. At the Maypole, I'd be watching people weigh stuff up. Butter was in a big slab with marble sides and a marble block at bottom. They used to get a piece out and pat it and bang it on top and leave a shape like a rose. And we got paint from Lamb's in Colliergate. You bought it loose, you'd take your own tin and threepence. Then the radio was battery driven. We'd get it topped up at Cussins and Light's. I was an Ovaltinie and I couldn't wait for Sunday evenings to put it on, the show for Ovaltinies. And Children's Hour, I wouldn't miss it for all the world.*

*We'd go swimming at St George's baths, if you swam your width, you got threepence, and if you did your length, you got sixpence. We used to flog ourselves to death. My mum came from Northumberland, and things were really bad so they were coming south. Her friends were in service and they'd come to our house on Friday night. We had a portable gramophone and they'd share coppers and buy records from Woolworth's. My dad would push the rug back and we would sit on the stairs while they danced. I remember two or three times we all went with the gramophone and my mother's ginger pop that she made herself, and sandwiches and a bat and ball, and walked to Clifton Ings.*

*I remember Pastor Hawkins at Elim Church. We'd go on Wednesday night and it was Sunshine Corner. He had no gas ring there, so mother boiled the kettles for tea. There was a billiard hall and auction room for carpets before they came. I still have a Bible from there. My mother's favourite word was, "Our Audrey will go". She said,*

*"Maggie* [a neighbour] *wants you". And Maggie said, "I want you to go to Uncle's". I hadn't a clue who Uncle was. It was Merriman's, the pawnshop, in Petergate. I had to go and stand in this queue. My dad nearly went mad when he heard but afterwards he saw the funny side 'cos I was so proud of me penny for going to Uncle's.*

Betty Powell was born,

*in Coffee Yard in 1930 at Gran and Grandad's house. Originally they came from Hungate. It was a terrible place. My Grandma had 13 children, 10 survived. Some went in the army in the First World War and never came back. They had awful lives them days. My mum was the youngest. Grandma used to take in washing and she was head*

*Betty Powell's mother Rosina Nelson and her brother posing for a French-polishing advertisement*
(Betty Powell)

*laundress at the Grange. The house in Coffee Yard was two up, two down. I can't remember anybody ever rowing or fighting down there. My Grandad was blind (from being a young boy) and we used to take him to the Black Bull, and stand with him at the corner, and somebody would come out and give him a chair. All the old men would sit there.*

*My mum was a waitress at Betty's and she'd leave me with my grandma. My grandma was a work horse, she really was. My brother [Terry] was born in Coffee Yard and he got polio when he was young. I remember taking him with his legs in irons. He was also in the fever hospital in an iron lung. But we'd play on the Minster steps and I'd take him in the pushchair. I could hear the organ music and hear the choir, I used to be there nearly all day.*

*Grandma Nelson, Betty Kirby, Pauline and Terry  Kirby, 1930s, Coffee Yard*
*(Betty Powell, née Kirby)*

*Once we were there, he'd just come out of hospital, he had plaster
on his leg and a big boot and this lady came up. She said, "I've been
watching you for quite a while. You're like a little mother to him.
Can I ask you where you live?" The lady was very tall and very well
dressed. About a fortnight later she came with this beautiful doll and a
train set for my brother. My mum was absolutely flabbergasted.*

*Later we lived at 2 Little Stonegate. And it had a huge yard. My brother
said he went down to the cellar and it had all these passages that went
to the Minster. My dad must have taken him down 'cos he couldn't
manage them steps. I remember a girl lived next door to us, she had a
lovely voice and played piano. They called her Biddy Passmore. I was
always in awe of her. She was such a lovely girl. She was always having
piano lessons or singing lessons.* [Biddy later became Trudy Luker,
and was internationally known as a singer and pianist].

*My Grandma had an ice cream stall, called Nelson's Ice Cream. She'd
be at the front where the toilets are* [St Sampson's Square] *in summer.
She'd park it in Hungate. We'd go on a Saturday night, I remember all
the stalls in the market, all lit up. I'd help her at six o'clock, wheel it
back to Hungate. I don't think we ate badly. She used to do scrag end of
mutton, in the oven, all crisp on top, abso-
lutely gorgeous. She always made Christmas
cake and Christmas pudding. My grandma
had two beautiful pictures on the wall above
the fire. One was Queen Victoria, and one was
a hansom cab with all horses and men in a
gold frame.*

*I'm sure Dr Dench came one or twice to
Little Stonegate. We had goosefat on if you
had a bad chest, or lint 'cos we got bronchitis.
All the houses would be damp. I remember
water running down the windows. If we had*

Dr Reg Dench c. 1950
*(York Oral History Society)*

*earache, she'd put on this stuff she'd done herself. I can't remember a
chemist anywhere. But doctors was a luxury. We still had Dr Dench
when we went to Horsman Avenue.*

*My dad was a singer, a tenor and he'd sing the 'Desert Song'. He had
a piano and had all this music, like 'Begin the Beguine'. I loved going
to Banks, looking at all the sheet music. My dad did all sorts apart
from professional singing. He worked on the railway, then had a taxi
business.*

*Sometimes my mother would pack us up with jam sandwiches and
potted meat and a bottle of lemonade or jug of tea, and we'd get the
train, get off at Scarborough and walk down the front. We'd sit on the
sands and we thought it was heaven.*

Malcolm Brown was born in 1941 in Leeman Road.

*On the night of the air raid in 1942, my mum dragged me down to
Swinegate where my granny lived. We were there on and off until
about 1950. That was my playground. There were not so many
people, a row of three houses where Gran lived in the centre. It is now
the Spanish place, and the Slug and Lettuce opposite. Mainly it was
the Gas Board and Myers and Burnell in the corner, a lot of fruit and
vegetable warehouses and lock up places.*

*The house was on three floors, with four bedrooms. Downstairs was
the front parlour used for special occasions, and an old aspidistra in
the window. Much of the living was done in the back parlour, with a
leaded fireplace and tiny scullery. That was the hub of the house. And
a tiny back yard, you could walk to the end in four or five strides, with
a tiny air raid shelter in the corner. When you came out of the back
door, directly opposite was the great big mangle for laundry day. On
Monday you couldn't get in the back parlour for drying clothes. And
she used to make brandy snap. My job was washing down the posser*

*Left: Malcolm Brown with his mother in Swinegate, looking towards Grape Lane (Jersey Dairy behind). Right: Brown family house in Back Swinegate; L-R, Flo Brown (Malcolm's mother), Uncle Jimmy, Granny Byworth, Aunt Betty and un-named girl at front.*

(Malcolm Brown)

*handle, so she could curl the brandy snap round it. She used the range and made her own bread. There was no going out buying things, they made it all. At one time there'd be nine living in that house, Great Granddad and Great Gran, Granddad and Gran and they had three children, and two brothers that never got married.*

*Opposite where Gran lived was a plumber's, a pub on the corner, then a back entrance to the doctors. Then coming back, a family called the Barkers, the printers which is now Border's, and a bookie's. There was the Jersey Dairy, almost opposite Elim. The entrance where wagons went was opposite the end of Back Swinegate. One of Gran's brothers was a fire watcher up on a roof top in the Second World War. The brothers would go in the Black Bull. Mother and her sister used to go in the back bedroom on a night and watch people coming out fighting, those who'd decided they'd had enough beer and wanted to be next world champion.*

41

*Malcolm Brown in Back Swinegate aged 3 or 4*
(Malcolm Brown)

*Malcolm's great grandparents,*
*Granny and Grandad Cox; Myers*
*and Burnell garage behind on left.*
(Malcolm Brown)

*Mr Ellis next door worked for the Yorkshire Post, they had an office in Swinegate. He used to make models and I remember one of a light-house. They had an Alsatian and it befriended me. It wasn't over noisy there but there'd always be something going on. We moved to Park Crescent in Monkgate but I counted both places as home. I spent a lot of time round there. I had a tricycle and I used to zoom around the streets and down the lanes. It was safe to play out. I was like the Lone Ranger, I can't remember anyone else of my age round there. That was my racetrack, my world. Really happy memories.*

## Chapter 3

# The Craftsmen

Historically, Stonegate is the street of craftsmen. In 1872, there were jewellers and silversmiths, wireworkers, a weaver, clock and watch-makers, engravers, cabinet makers, glaziers, woodcarvers and gilders, glass stainers, upholsterers, artists, bookbinders, a hatter, piano manu-facturers, a lamp maker, printers, boot and shoe makers, composi-tors, a stonemason and a blacking manufacturer. Over the years, most of these disappeared. By the 1960s, there were still craftsmen in the street, as well as neighbouring Swinegate and Grape Lane. But a mass exodus took place in the 1970s when Stonegate was made a foot street, and when property rents became too high. Today almost all of these crafts have gone.

## The Wood Carver

The name of Dick Reid is synonymous with restoration and conserva-tion in York. His work has extended way beyond the city. The York Civic Trust Report of 2003 lists just a few of his projects; the recreation of a whole 18th century ceiling based on the evidence of one *Country Life* photograph, a series of exquisite marble fireplaces for Lord Roth-schild at Spencer House, and the superb pair of overdoors fashioned by the deaf and dumb carver Martin Dutton for Fairfax House. At one stage in the 1990s, his was the largest carving workshop in England with five wood and five stone carvers, plus masons, cabinet makers, gilders and allied outworkers. Dick has carved figures for the National Museum of Wales, the memorial to Richard Dimbleby in Westminster Abbey, eight 10 foot high columns in the restoration of the temple at Studley Royal. Craftsmen from his workshop have carved the stone urn on the grave of Princess Diana and the carving of her name on the temple at Althorp, as well as the statues at St Mungo's Church

*Dick Reid in his workshop* (Dick Reid)

in Glasgow and many other churches and well-known buildings. He was given an honorary doctorate of the University of York in 2002. Dick recalls his beginnings,

> *I was born in 1934 in Newcastle and I came to the Shambles as a carver in 1958. Steve Harrison had his shop there. I would carve rose bowls and they would be sold in the shop. That activity went on until the elm tree disappeared from the face of England. Elm was wonderful but once elm disease came, the wood became rarer and rarer. You can use oak but it's not a suitable wood and chestnut's rare. The wood turners have all disappeared, it has become automated. If I'd stayed in Newcastle, the work would have come in because of the reputation of the studio. So I had to teach for a number of years till I slowly got known.*

*I trained as a wood and stone carver. Because of the space you need to carve stone, it was some years before that started. I carved bowls to make a living and house name signs, keeping a studio in Stonegate, teaching during the day and working evenings and weekends.*

*The studio was rather cramped, on the third storey in Stonegate, and Greenwood's were developing the back of their properties, fronting onto Grape Lane. I'd done one or two jobs on the antique restoration side. I moved into Grape Lane on a three year lease and that was when the workshop started to grow. The properties were very extensive. Number 19 is a restaurant now but was a derelict property then and an old lady was living in the end. I had an entrance into a yard with an old chapel. They demolished that and made a car park. Bodies were buried there, so there was conflict but it was resolved. A lorry with five tons of concrete came. It backed onto what is the back of Barley Hall,*

*Dick Reid's workshop (Dick Reid)*

*and an old studio, Knowles. It was fascinating, 'cos all the glass and tools of Knowles's studio were still there. I took over the storeroom in Coffee Yard and eventually bought 3 and 5 Grape Lane, two cottages, the next one down was a printer's who ran round the back and had an entrance in Petergate,* [Quacks].

*Putting it into historical context, modernism after the war became popular. It was creeping into church furnishing and there wasn't much work there. The traditional work for wood carvers was thin on the ground and studios were closing all over and in fact the effect on craftsmanship in the '50s and '60s was disastrous and many traditional arts and crafts disappeared. Trying to keep a studio going was extremely difficult. I'd moved into doing lettering for honours boards and the like, which took me into church work and it was an introduction to Anelay's the builders and Francis Johnson the architect, that started my career. Then the Dean put a minute in the Diocesan Advisory Committee that 'Dick Reid's work was acceptable and to be recommended'. So suddenly all the architectural plans that came up, I was able to become involved with.*

*I was slowly building up a collection of work. At that time there was a demand for antique restoration, but it needed to be in conjunction with cabinet makers. Rod Dunning, whose father was the great dance band leader Derek Dunning, moved upstairs and had a cabinet making shop. I had my wood carving shop on the first floor and machinery on the ground floor. Greenwood the antique dealer was our principal customer. Life was great and there was masses of work. Church work was a bonus on top. By that time I was working with firms like Anelay's, Hunter and Smallpage, and Heppell's in Aldwark and restoring antiques. Then the great entrepreneur, Alan Robertson, came along from Discovery Antiques, and opened a little antique shop in Minster Gates, and we restored his work. Andrew Podmore who'd trained as a French polisher with Hunter and Smallpage, came back and he moved in downstairs. So we had three craftsmen there. In*

## *The Bookbinder*

Charles Symington was born in Harrogate, came to York in 1962 and joined his father Douglas as a bookbinder ten years later.

*At home there were always piles of books. I remember as a child, being in an attic and building books, making a fort,' cos there were thousands of books around.*

*We worked in Petergate in 1974* [at the corner of Stonegate]. *The building belonged to Hardcastle the jeweller and someone bought it and wanted to refurbish the whole lot. We went to Coffee Yard in 1985. It was sublet from Godfrey's bookshop, Richardson the baker owned that building, except for the toilet, that was rented from the*

*Charles (left) and Douglas Symington, c. 1984*

(Charles Symington)

Bishop of Durham. Godfrey's had moved out except for a room on the ground floor where they stored a lot of second hand books, surplus to requirements.  It used to be a coffee house in the 1700s and underneath the rooms, you could go down to the cellars where they roasted coffee beans. We started out with some equipment that my dad bought in 1932, from the Black Swan in Coney Street, that was a printer's and a bindery. My father borrowed £50 from his grandfather and bought the bindery for £100. And he sold half of the lead weights for £50, so he got the whole bindery for £50.

There'd been printing in Stonegate area for years. The bookbinding would be a different sort of place. Often with the great bookbinders in France, the printer would print it up into boards and they would take it to the bookbinder and they would bind it in leather or cloth.

I would get there at nine and work through till eight at night. The Ghost Walk would go past, there was always a ghoul or ghost jumping out at people. And there were no lights down there. Grape Lane had a history with so many murders.  Was it once Grope Lane?

Downstairs on the right hand side was the guillotine and the card room. Then I would have a bench near a window. I'd the binding basically in one room. We had a blocking room separately upstairs for any gold work or tooling, as upstairs was quite quiet. You need to be on your own to do that kind of work. There were eight bookbinders in York when I first started with my father, and plenty of work. The Press had their own bookbinder, Rusholme Printers had their own, and Coward's. Wood and Richardson's had June who worked in King's Square. We did all the gold for them but she bound the books.

I seemed to do the work and my dad used to talk. He said he'd be back in five minutes but I never could keep track of him, he liked to be in the know of what was happening in the area, he had the gift of talking. Dick Reid was in Grape Lane, and Noel Beech, and another bookbinder, Dick Smith, in Grape Lane, the printers Noel Richard-son's, and a lot of crafts people in the area. He'd go to Kilvington's, the ironmongers, Januirek at Godfrey's, and he used to see Nigel, the bookseller at Minster Gates. We did loads and loads of books for Godfrey's actually. There was another chap, Vic Mort, he's 90 now, he ran the picture framing business in Grape Lane. He used to sell facsimiles of old prints and maps. Another place was a newspaper shop, Mrs Dakin, whose husband was a prisoner of war in a Japanese camp. She ran this little shop for years. Gary Greenwood, he took over his father's antique shop. My father knew them way back when they lived in Harrogate. The trouble was getting through the work then. Much more than what you could cope with. I did work for the Minster Library and I knew a couple of people at the Glazier's Trust, Keith Hilton and Peter Gibson in Minster Yard, the stained glass man.

For the city I restored Drake's York, 'Eboracum' in two volumes, of 1636, and it was the author's copy. There's a huge portrait in the Mansion House where he's giving these copies to the council. When they found them, they were very disbound. It was shown to visitors for 246 years so was beginning to fall to pieces. The leather binding had dried out and cracked and a number of plates were torn. We spent three weeks restoring it. It was unique because it has the original portrait of the artist and is one of two or three copies which were hand coloured. I had to be very careful taking dirt off the gold leaf. In restoring books, we do not add new materials if we can help it but restore what is already there. If it is looked after properly there is no reason why it shouldn't last another 250 years.

I've always done work for Lord Halifax, Castle Howard, National Trust properties, York Archaeological Trust, Peter Anelay the builders, Ampleforth [College], and well-known people in York that have libraries. I've done remembrance books in nearly every church in the area. We did a lot of work for a place at Clifton Moor, Maxiprint, and work for Noel Richardson and Linden Richardson. My dad used to *travel a lot, and would deliver books to Raymond Burton of Burton's. He lived in Whitwell Hall with a big library. In those days, I would be doing between 18 and 20 books a week.*

*There's a very wide range of restoration work and preservation. We do all sorts of bindings, cloth, calf and morocco. The materials came from a company in Edinburgh, J Hewitt and Sons. They're the best leather in the world and they supply everything the bookbinder needs. The main exporter is America. But Ratchford's the cloth people are in Stockport. And Hall in Norwich, they do lovely marble papers.*

*Probably the most expensive was a Martin Luther book, owned by a man who owned a baseball team in America and I rebound it in full leather. It was printed in about 1460, worth about £10,000. I restored it and it's in a vault in America for ever.*

*It was a gradual thing* [pedestrianisation]. *Deangate closed and they were slowly closing street by street, and eventually it was limited to mornings or late afternoons for deliveries of materials. People with books, a heavy commodity, wouldn't bring them in. So I kept driving out collecting work but I wouldn't get the work done. There was a protest against the council because of the restrictions, and all of us got together but it didn't get anywhere. I couldn't afford to stay there, the rents were huge. We moved out* [to Hospital Fields Road in 1989]. *All the craftsmen rented and they all moved. It wasn't just the council rents that had gone up, it was the church, York Minster as well,' cos they owned a lot of property down there.*

Douglas Symington died in 1994 but Charles still continues his work in Bishopthorpe Road.

*It's a vocation. I like doing it. It's creating something out of nothing, and a certain style that you have. All bookbinders recognise their own books.*

## The Watch and Clockmakers

### The Kleiser Dynasty

Andrew and Joseph Kleiser were brothers from Baden in Germany. Andrew who was born in 1820, came to England in 1840 and started out working for Philip Schwerer at 38 Stonegate. He bought the business in 1842 with Augustine Kleiser. Schwerer returned to Germany but his brother Matthew, with whom he had initially traded in Petergate, continued at 18 Stonegate. Joseph came over in the 1850s and joined Andrew. They advertised as 'clock and watchmakers, silversmiths, jewellers and opticians. Importers of novelties in clocks from France and Germany'. Andrew married Hannah Potter and became naturalised in October 1853. They had three sons, Cuthbert, John and Louis, but their only daughter Jane died at the age of five. Joseph married Mary Potter from Osbaldwick in 1854.

Andrew and Joseph's shop was in the premises now occupied by Little Betty's. There is a passage at the side of the shop with a well-painted metal plate bearing the name Kleiser's Court. In the 19th century there were a few dwellings down there. Their relative Otmar Kleiser was a watchmaker in Parliament Street and the two businesses were affiliated. By 1861, the Stonegate shop employed one man, Jonas Haffner. Within ten years, the brothers were employing three men and two boys, Andrew's son Cuthbert being an apprentice. In 1851, Andrew's younger brother

*Kleiser's Court, off Stonegate (Lesley Collett)*

*View up Stonegate, date unknown: shop sign for M. Wehrly and M. Kleiser can be seen at right. (Mike Race)*

Martin Kleiser, aged 18, had stayed with the family but within a few years had set up on his own at 14 Stonegate, buying the business from Matthew Schwerer. There must have been some feud as Andrew and Joseph included their following in their advertising,

> *'Kleiser. 39 Stonegate and Parliament Street. The only two establishments carried on by Messrs Kleiser, and there are no other firms of this name. The public and their customers are respectfully cautioned against being misled by seeing the name of Kleiser elsewhere where no such person exists'.*

Otmar Kleiser who had started the Parliament Street business died in 1866 and his wife Louisa continued there until her remarriage in 1874. By 1881 M Kleiser of 12 Stonegate was succeeded by Matthew Wehrly & Co. who were advertising:

*M WEHRLY & CO*
*(late M Kleiser & Co)*
*Watch and clock makers*
*Jewellers, silversmiths and opticians,*
*Every description of repairs promptly and properly executed*
*By skilful workmen on the premises*
*Guinea gold wedding rings*
*Importer of French, German and American clocks*

Wehrly was in partnership with Severin Heine, employing one man and two apprentices. He had gone by 1891 and the business was run by Roman Wehrly and Heine. This was part of what is now Mulberry Hall and the shop and sign are featured on many commercial post-cards of the early 1900s.

Andrew and Joseph both died in 1885 and they and their families lie in adjacent graves with identical headstones, so it was a harmonious partnership to the last.

*Gravestones of Andrew and Joseph Kleiser* (Van Wilson)

The Stonegate shop closed and the business moved fully to Parliament Street. Hannah Kleiser died in 1898 but their descendants remained in the city until 1929. Cuthbert's son, Louis Cyril Kleiser, became a soldier in the First World War, although there was still hostility to Germans in the city and shops with German sounding names had their windows broken.

Victorian Stonegate must have rung with the sound of foreign accents as there were also Italian jewellers in the vicinity, such as Joseph Fattorini who was a watchmaker at 18 Stonegate in the 1850s. The last reminder of the Kleisers is a clock in the Council Chamber of the Guildhall which bears the words 'Kleiser of York'.

## *The Jeweller*

Adrian Gell was born in York in 1933 and became an apprentice watchmaker.

*I started at Grant's next door to Woolworth's, and my first week's wage was nine shillings, which after seven years became 30 shillings at the age of 21. When I first went to the interview, I walked into the room and I don't know how I stood it, just one mass of clocks ticking. The noise was out of this world. It was a cacophony. All the walls were full of clocks and watches hung on boards on hooks. But after I'd been there a while, if I'd done a particular clock, I could actually just listen to that clock. You would never have believed you could talk amongst that noise, but after that you never heard it, the brain just accepts it.*

*Not only was it in the clock and watch side, I was also taught the jewellery side, making rings and also repairs. Life was good and very interesting. Then I was called up into the forces and I met Arthur, who'd also been an apprentice in York in the watch trade, and we decided we'd keep together after we came out. At the time, Inglis's of Stonegate was*

*Adrian Gell, 1972* (Adrian Gell)

*starting a workshop up, so Arthur and myself set up the repair business for him. It was a good shop, well known, they covered most aspects of the jewellery and watch trade, so we always had plenty of work. We met other jewellers in York, and in the street there was Mr Veal and Hardcastle's at the top. There was a certain something about everybody there, it was closely knit. Being in the workshops we had to do so much on the shop side, meeting customers, telling them what was wrong and what they should do about it. We had a little lift where they could bring the watches and clocks up to me instead of going downstairs for them. I had a boxer dog which loved playing with the big 14 pound grandfather clock weights on the floor of the workshop, but of course someone underneath, trying to buy a lovely diamond ring for his lady, would hear this rumbling all the time of this dog. After a short time Arthur decided to leave and set up on his own.*

*David Inglis was in the shop with some ladies and a gentleman helping. His father was in New Street, he had an optician's, so I used to do repairs to glasses for him. The Inglis family was a big family in York.* [James Brown Inglis, jeweller and optician, was Lord Mayor in 1922 and a long time councillor].

*Edward, Prince of Wales, walking with the Lord Mayor, Alderman Inglis on 31st May 1923.*

(Image reproduced courtesy of City of York Council, Local Studies Collection)

*They dealt with all sorts of jewellery, watches, clocks, handbags, expensive ones, all sorts of baggage, and pearls of course which we had to repair. I worked from half past eight to six o'clock at night. In winter time, with Christmas coming up, we were open till eight often. Wages were never marvellous but because you were in the jewellery trade, people thought you had plenty of money. You spent a lot of time repairing watches quickly so they could go on holiday and they would go on the beach and get sand in and stop them again. When you're dealing with lords and ladies of big houses, a clock was very important*

*in the room. You had beautiful furniture there and the clock was often bought specifically to go with the rest of the room. You just had to make sure you repaired it properly so it would always keep right. We'd get £2.10s for repairing a grandfather clock which nowadays would be an arm and a leg.*

*A lot of the clocks would be in turrets on the top. They were very heavy, like a church clock, with big long weights which went up and down. On one occasion we brought one from Lord Feversham's and we had to go up a special staircase instead of the large one in the hall, to get to the tower. He was having guests this particular time and we were taking this big clock back up to the tower. One of the apprentices was carrying the cast iron weight, 18 inches by about a foot. And we got to the door when it opened up onto the main hallway where all these people were coming in, and he dropped it and it landed on my toe. There were exclamations and things like that, but we quickly picked up this weight and disappeared up into the tower as quickly as possible. They often used to let us have a drink of home made cider that they made on the premises. We weren't looked down upon. We were a class which they needed to do the work, so we were respected.*

*Once you made a name for yourself with that particular family, they would keep you forever. In the ordinary world, you would get somebody coming in and they wanted a watch for work, then gradu-ally they'd be courting, so they wanted an engagement ring. Then a wedding ring, then a canteen of cutlery. Then they had children, and got silver pushers for food and little dishes for them. They were very loyal usually, if you did it right for them. When they bought a wedding ring, they were often given a small fish knife and fork set.*

*As an apprentice, it was hard. It wasn't like nowadays with central heating, all we had was a coal fire. Every little part* [of the watch or clock] *you had to brush with a long thin brush, which you rubbed on a block of white chalk. And you had to clean it in spirit and brush every part to get them nice and bright and shiny. You'd be holding the part in tissue and then all of a sudden, oops, it would fly off and some-times land in the ashes in the fire. So then it was a hands and knees job, looking for all these parts. So tempers frayed, that type of thing used to happen frequently. You had to make sure all the holes in the plates were beautifully clean or it could make everything slow down. We didn't have machines, they came later. There's machines that do timing for you now. You can put the movement on a big electronic machine and it would tell you if it was gaining or losing, whereas we'd hang everything up on hooks in different positions and you'd regulate it according to how it was doing.*

*We had a man who supplied spare parts for us and tools for the trade, in St Martin's Lane. He said, "Are you a new lad at the game?" "Yes I've come for some tools. I need eyeglasses, how much are they?" "Well from 2/6d to several pounds". "Could I have a 2/6d one please?" "No you can't, you have the best, because your eyes deterio-rate if you have cheap stuff. Always have a proper lens". He also said, "Do you realise now you've entered the trade, you'll either become one of the hardest swearing men in York or you'll go completely mad?"*

*I remember going to an old lady's, I sent a chap down who was working for us, and he brought the clock, repaired it and took it back and we got a notification that it had gone wrong. It was a little pendulum clock on a wall. He went back, started it up again, then got another notification. This went on about five times and the last time we got a complaint was that he'd been looking through the side of the clock, and he'd put his brylcreem on the wallpaper. We then had to decorate it, it wasn't good enough to just do that part, we had to have the room re-papered. Then we got a complaint it had stopped again so I went this time and brought it back to work. I couldn't understand it because we could never find anything really bad, and then I took it back. The lady was out and her sister came to the door. "Oh have you brought that thing back again? I wish you hadn't. It's me who's*

*and before 1682 it was used for abbots and bishops who were coming presumably to the Minster. It's a little area, not even as big as a room.*

*My grandfather's father was a painter and decorator. His brother took that on and grandfather went to art school. He just suddenly got an interest, went down to London and trained with a firm called Playton and Bell. I think he was only down there about a year then he came back and started up on his own. His work took off and he got busy. He had leaflets printed. The first one was a very small card, 1859 or 1861, the first forays into stained glass in his early 20s. On the leaflets he describes himself in different ways – art stainer, stained glass artist, ecclesiastical decorator. It was a place people went to, to talk about stained glass. They had candles and all sorts of church things.*

*They had six children and a maid. I remember the maid who lived downstairs, Sarah. She used to come on her bike, cook dinner in the*

*John Alder Knowles* (Jill Murray)

*cellar, and bring it up the stone steps with no banister. The main
staircase went up to the attic. At the back where the workshops were,
was another flight of stairs up to the sewing room. They had girls
sewing antimacassars and anything you wanted for the church. And
my aunts were excellent embroiderers and my grandmother was very
good. There were four girls. They all went to art school. One aunt
stayed there, she never got married. One aunt got married and went
away, one had a tearoom in Poppleton, and the other had a shop in
Petergate. They had a kiln in the passage at the side of the house. The
cottages were behind that and they had the door knocked into them, so
that we had a back entrance into Coffee Yard.*

*At Christmas we used to go, they always had a big party. They would
think of wonderful things for children, like massive crackers they
strung across the room. My uncle was a very good amateur conjuror
and used to do tricks. They had a piano. We were all very musical, and
they were all big theatre goers and big readers.*

John Ward Knowles, and then his two sons, would get commissions to
do stained glass windows, as far afield as Carrickfergus in Northern
Ireland.

*And they restored the St William window and the St Cuthbert
window in the Minster. He ordered paints from France and Belgium.*
[He also obtained pigments from France, Italy and the Nether-
lands]. *The glass used to go everywhere on the train. It was packed
in crates, collected by the railway and delivered, and then somebody
would go and actually put the windows in. I think they would get a
faculty. If people are commissioning a window, they have an idea of
what they want.*

They also did joinery, with ecclesiastical overtones, with painted
woodwork at the back.

*Stained glass in 35 Stonegate today* (Christine Kyriacou)

*Then my grandfather was getting very elderly and maybe a bit muddled. My father was still quite young. But my father died in '51, whereas my uncle carried on the business on his own. During the war there was no work. They spent their time taking the stained glass out of churches and after the war they were busy putting it all back in again. My father just trained at home. By the time he was old enough and he'd got out of art school, he had to work in the business. He did the window in St Cuthbert's Chapel on Farne Island. I remember him saying he had to go out in this rowing boat and if it was bad weather, he couldn't get there. They did the heraldic panels at Bishopthorpe Palace. My father did quite a lot of altar carving. And then after he died, they decided they'd let the shop. The workrooms got into a worse and worse state. Eventually we sold the workrooms and the chapel* [in Grape Lane, see chapter on churches].

*My grandfather used to collect clocks. You went in and you never heard anything from the street. All you could hear were these hundreds of clocks, it was a very atmospheric house. This old man who worked for my grandfather, he was Irish, said he definitely used to see my grandfather coming, after he had died, he used to see him in the workrooms.*

Jill left York for some time, but then returned to Stonegate

*in 1974, and it was still Victorian, those geyser things in the bath, lino on the floors and no central heating. My aunt lived there on her own till she was in her 90s and she had a stroke and died. And that's when we moved in. We had central heating installed, a phone installed, the whole building was just falling down. We had a lot of work done to it. We had a planning officer who just about lived with us. It was very strict, grade 2 \*. We had parts rebuilt but you've got to use the old materials, you've got to use oak even if that oak isn't going to be visible, they won't let you put in another type of wood. There was a joiner doing a job for us and he remembered my father and my uncle and said you could never rush them. You could go in and calmly they were doing this job.*

*We made a living for 25 years. It was called Number 35, selling cards, art postcards, posters. After a few years, we were approached by one of our suppliers who asked us to take over his business, distributing art cards for museums and galleries like the National Gallery.*

## The Wire Workers

The Kilvington family business of wireworkers was one of the oldest in Stonegate. Charles became the first wireworker, based in Walmgate. His grandsons, Charles and Benjamin came to 10 Stonegate and started the business there in 1838. Charles worked as a glass and china shopkeeper in the firm and Ben was the wire worker. Ben died in 1923, by which time his two sons, George and Walter, had joined the business. George Kilvington was apprenticed to Thomas Green of 22 Stonegate, next door to the bookshop 'The Sign of the Bible'. Once Kilvington opened his own shop, it eventually occupied what

*Ben Kilvington with Mary Ann's wire chair in his premises at 13 Stonegate.*

Reproduced from book "Ben Kilvington & Company", 1989, published by Sessions of York.

*George Kilvington*
*(Martin Boyd)*

had once been three timber framed houses. In 1872 number 11 Stonegate was added to his premises, and in 1897, number 9 was bought. It had been owned by Sarah Bean, an umbrella maker, in 1828 and changed hands eight times before it was bought by Kilvington's. In 1867 George Kilvington was advertising wiring of window blinds, greenhouses and conservatories, iron and wire fencing, archways, garden chairs, aviaries, game, poultry and sparrow proof netting, and wire work for church, dairy and granary windows. He also stocked corn sieves, gardeners' riddles and German enamelled canary and parrot cages. The shop was also the agent for Green's Patent Mowing Machines. Thomas Green's advertisement offered such weird and wonderful items as beetle traps, dormouse cages, dickeys for sifting oatmeal, chair springs, horse muzzles, wire for bottling soda water and 'improved grates for willies'.

Walter had two sons, Gordon, who became a journalist, and Benjamin (Ben) who continued as wireworker in Stonegate from the 1940s. He was Master of the Gild of Freemen of York in 1972, and founded the Stonegate Traders' Association. Unfortunately his only son Simon Benjamin, born in 1957, died in his 30s, and when Ben died, he was the last of the line. At the corner of the shop is a timber post with a 17th century figurehead, the bust of a seafaring lady. Dick Reid repaired this in the 1970s, a restoration which took three years.

David Simpson worked at Kilvington's in 1953 when he was 15.

*I started work in short trousers. There was the shop and a small factory in Little Stonegate, a long building 30-40 metres long, with double storeys and double doors. Next door was Theakston's Plumbers.*

*I was there for three years then joined the army. It was just when health and safety were coming into industry. Machines would run with safety belts flying around, they started to have machinery guards when I was there. Fred Weir, the foreman, could do anything with a piece of wire. He was one of those people that left a good impression. These things that they bend with aluminium wire on Blackpool beach, like a motorbike, a novelty, he could do it. He knew the business inside out. He was there about 40 years. About eight or nine worked in the factory, Fred Weir, Ben and George Kilvington, the Adamson brothers, a chap called Taylor, and Joe Drake, who became a professional rugby player, and Ronnie Gee worked in the shop. It was strict, you had to be there on time, you didn't take days off or leave early. When you started you had to light the fire, wash up, make tea, get cigarettes and matches for the older chaps at the cigarette kiosk opposite Inglis the jewellers. One guy would count the matches in the box, between 48 and 52, we'd take a few out to wind him up. Practically everybody smoked then, including me. I earned the equivalent of £1.20 in today's money. I think we worked 46 to 48 hours. There were no facilities. The toilet and that was it, no hot water, and some of the cups we had, you wouldn't even drink out of today.*

*There was the printer's opposite, Noel Richardson. We'd all play football in the street with them. They still had horses and carts then. The*

*Walter Harrison and David Simpson, 1951-2. (David Simpson)*

*Co-op delivered milk and they delivered coal by cart, before electric vans. Kilvington's had a big hand cart to deliver things in the city.*

*George Kilvington was about 65 or 66, born in the 1800s, a strict upbringing, he lived through two world wars. He was not very tall, five foot eight at the most, but a solid chap. He made you toe the line, in those days you had respect for people. You wouldn't ask questions, you'd do as you were told. Everything was hand made apart from welding sets. We had people wanting wire net for a rabbit cage, chain link to put round gardens, tennis court surrounds. Most of the lamp posts had baskets with flowers. We had the contract with the Council to make those, both high up and at ground level. And long wastepaper baskets for schools. They had electric saws and electric guillotines, but Kilvington's didn't move with the times. They just plodded on. I went back to see them about 1960 and things hadn't changed.*

*We had our times of fun but didn't really have time for much. Denis Lawson liked fishing and he'd arrange fishing matches for us, we'd go off to Stamford Bridge on our bikes for a tournament. Everybody rode bikes into work. Where the double doors were, we parked the bikes in there. The bottom storey was for materials, the welding set and guillotine. It was lit by four 40 watt bulbs, the roof had glass panels. The machinery was on the second floor, with two looms for weaving the wire. It was always busy, you never sat around.*

Mandy Cryer was born in 1921, and came to York during the war. She recalls Kilvington's.

*I knew Ben. We used to congregate in the Starre before I was married. I went to Kilvington's and said, "I could do with a hood [for her daughter's pram], and would you make me one?" It was a hood that came up and down. In those days bicycles had flat carriers and you had to tie things on. And I wanted a wire basket that I could put cereal packets in. Kilvington's were very obliging. You can't do that now, have things made personally.*

Denis Lawson started there in 1943.

*I was 14½. I worked for Walter. His son Ben was in the workshop and took the business over when Walter died. He was a good rugby player, he used to play for Yorkshire. When we'd go on these away jobs, doing tennis courts, we'd go all over, and when we had our sandwich, he'd always get out and have a game of rugby. You couldn't stop him, he'd cut through the lot of us like a dose of salts. Real big strong lad he was. We had a joiner's shop at the back. There was a passageway in Little Stonegate, and down this were three or four rundown workshops. Walter was always out of the shop watching. He took a big pride in this ship's lady stuck on the corner. Two or three cars damaged it over the years. It was repaired each time. Walter used to get the number and send them the bill.*

*Former ship's figurehead on the cornerpost of Kilvington's shop*
(Lesley Collett)

*guillotine. I have three mount machines, I had a heat sealer, a big flat bed press. Prior to that when I did a job for Rowntree's, they brought a heat press out of their advertising department. One of these big wheel things. They were going through a nostalgia trip, I used to get all their advertising, tin tops, and different chocolate boxes. They had a load of print stuff and I put them onto block mounts. The garage was full of block boards, 3000 of them. It took 18 months to do.*

*I bought a mount cutter, the first one that was invented. It was £139, it was extortionate. Mount cutters were from America, or some from Germany. You find in industries, most machinery is from abroad. Same as in the print shop, all the machines were French, Italian, Japanese.*

*Then eventually it started to wear out. And I had this brainwave. I decided to buy a new one but cut this one in half for the small mounts. The front of the plate was worn out so I chopped it in half and brought everything forward. It's a long thin piece of board, about 40 inches long, and running down the middle is a metal plate with a cutter. Two years later we went to the trade fair, there they were on one of the stalls, small mount cutters. I said to one of the reps, "Where's this come from?" He said, "It was your idea". They'd actually made a small version.*

Noel left Grape Lane in 1999 and now works from home.

## *The Joiner*

Arthur Dodd was born in 1933 in York and was an apprentice from 14 to 21 at,

*J Hodsman and son, joiners and undertakers, Eldon Street in the Groves. I got £1.2s.6d when I started. When I came out, it was about £7 a week. They were only a small firm but a good quality firm. We'd do a lot of architectural work.*

*In about 1953, wintertime, I was working on roofs, putting new box gutters in, (I suppose they were that old, they were going rotten), and replacing roof spars in Stonegate. It was all connected, the roofs, you can go more or less the full length of Stonegate, just one side, from Banks Music Shop down to Pawson's the rubber shop. In the roofs all the doors were left open.*

*There'd be at least eight different trades all working. The plumbers would be Frank Hall's from the Groves. Bricklayers was Tom Watson's at Heworth, they were the main contractors, and Hargreaves tilers, or it could have been Shouksmith's plumbers. We worked with many different small firms.*

*Over the years we did do a few things there. I remember finding a coin when I was repairing skirting at Brown's tailors, next to Pawson's, and I gave the coin to the shop owner, he was interested. At Godfrey's, they bought a shop next door, and I put all the shelves in. There was an optician's next door to Brown's. They were going to make an upstairs room, a consulting room. It was all old fashioned panelling and we were going to put modern sheeting round. I put timber round the edge and the sheeting on and then they didn't get permission. So all what I'd done had to be pulled out.*

*We were just doing internal things, we never did any shop fronts. We could have done it if we'd been asked, but we weren't considered shop fitters. We did quite a lot of work at Banks Music Shop over the years but Miss Banks couldn't see the job till it was done. You'd finish something and she'd want it pulling down and altering. We built a little office inside, all of wood and we'd make cupboards for storing things in. They used to keep all the sheet music up in t'roof. I remember working at Miss Banks's house at Poppleton. She had quite a big field. They would keep horses on it and had do's in her field. Probably for the scouts and things.*

*I was with the firm until it closed in the '60s. I went to Shepherd's and worked at the Minster for five years. There was a big construction job. I dug it down about fifteen foot and put new footings right round on the east end. We also put a new roof on the main tower. The undercroft was all dug out 'cos that was new concrete underneath the main tower to support, they had to put pressure pads all over till the concrete got settled then they'd fill it with grout. They could only do so much at a time, obviously couldn't strip out everything. We used to make coffins and I'd go with the boss to put people in them. And I also did the carrying at churches.*

## The Milliner

Women's businesses in the area tended to be mainly dressmakers, milliners, needleworkers and artists. In the 1880s, Emmeline Dent was a dressmaker at number 15 Stonegate, Elizabeth Underwood was an artificial florist at number 50, Emma Morrell was also a dressmaker at number 54. The Misses Mary and Jane Middleton were artists at number 7, Louisa Huggins was a dressmaker at number 35 from the 1890s to the 1920s and Mrs Heselgrave was a watchmaker at number 40. By the 1930s, Monique the dressmaker was at number 2, May Harrison was a ladies' hatter at number 5, and Margaret Perry a dressmaker and costumier at number 35. Madame Ernestica was a milliner at number 45.

Joan Whitwell was born in 1930, and went to work for Ethel's Milliners at 5 Stonegate when she was 16.

*Ethel, Mrs Broadbent, had a big house on Hull Road which she divided into three flats. They came from the Manchester area. He* [her husband] *had a business painting and decorating and taught at the Art School. To his amazement, she saw this shop and opened it. My mum used to go and clean her flat. And she said, "I need a girl to train". So I went and she paid me the princely sum of £1.10s which was a fortune in those days. Every birthday I got £1 rise. She would have a week in Blackpool every year and I had to look after the shop. I got extra payment for that. She taught me millinery, and how to trim and shape with steam. It was quite busy at race times, wealthy people would bring whatever they were wearing and wanted a hat to go with it. She would do her best and would go especially to buy something in the colour and the shade of the outfit. She trimmed hats with osprey feathers. All the older ladies wore hats in those days. She had a good clientele. She taught me dressmaking and about calcium for my nails.*

# Chapter 4
# The Booksellers and Printers

Stonegate has been the home of booksellers and printers for centuries. At the top of the street, on the corner of Minster Gates (called Bookbinder's Alley at one time), there is still the statue of Minerva, the Roman goddess of wisdom and drama, sitting beside a pile of books with an owl and a theatrical mask. The bookseller William Tesseyman operated at Minster Gates at the 'Sign of the Crown' between 1760 and 1801. In 1801 John Wolstenholme took over and moved to the corner, the premises becoming the 'Sign of the Book', and it was at this time that Minerva was erected there, designed by his cousin Francis Wolstenholme. The York Book Club met in the building, and Wolstenholme also began to publish the Yorkshire Gazette in 1819.

*Figure of Minerva in Minster Gates. (Lesley Collett)*

## *Minster Gates Books*

At the beginning of the 20th century there were no booksellers in Minster Gates but in more recent times, there were two bookshops. In the 1930s, Edwin Story, whose main shop was at Micklegate Bar, ran premises at number 9. After the Second World War, Pickering's bookshop operated there before moving to the Shambles. Minster Gates Books was opened by Christopher Holt in 1970. Today the shop is at number 10, with several rooms of books on three floors, as well as a room of maps and prints, concentrating on illustrations from 1800 to 1940. The bookshop is owned by Nigel Wallace. As a graduate in the early 1970s, Nigel was living in Weymouth.

*I walked into a shop which was half antiques, half books. The antique dealer had just bought up the stock of a second hand bookseller and then realized that books were going a lot slower than antiques. So when I enthused about some books I'd found, he said, "You can buy the whole stock if you want". That was about 20,000 books for £1000 and it seemed a real bargain. I borrowed the money to buy the books except I had nowhere to put them. My parents had bought a house to retire to in York and they said I could put the books in there for a while. So I moved 20,000 books from Weymouth to York. I then panicked and walked round the second hand bookshops here and asked if anyone wanted to buy 20,000 books. I walked into Minster Gates and I don't think he was doing well. We came to an arrangement where we would go into partnership and I would move half my books in and we would share the takings. It didn't work very well and for the first year or so, I realized it wasn't going to support both of us. York wasn't very touristy. He decided he would go if I took over his overdraft. I moved in the other half of my books and gradually paid it off. It took a long time to get the business going and to learn it 'cos I knew nothing at that time. I was interested in literature and in books but didn't know much about their value. I really had to just pick it up on my own.*

*Minster Gate Bookshop (Van Wilson)*

*You think as you get better at a job, gradually you're going to free-wheel as you get older. That seemed to be the case up to about 1998 when bookselling on the internet really started to get going in America particularly. Then a lot of second hand booksellers realised, that we were going to relearn a lot of things, because in the past you could rely on your knowledge and experience to value books. The internet is the perfect economic model where you've got supply and demand there for everybody to see, and however good a book is, if there's not enough people wanting it, the price starts to go down as another bookseller puts another copy on. It's made some books more desirable and a lot easier to sell. And it's made some books extremely hard to sell.*

*In about 1985 we realised there were quite a lot of bookshops in York and we ought to be selling it. You'd begun to get Hay on Wye doing well having established itself as a book town and the idea was that we could start to sell York as a book town. We organised a few weekends with lecture tours, but there was a shortage of booksellers with time to go on organising it. Now all we do is the pamphlet with a list of bookshops.*

*The idea was that you used your knowledge to put a group of books together and somebody could then come and find lots of books on that subject. Now anybody can go on the internet and find virtually any book. In the late '80s and '90s, a lot of booksellers were putting collections together to sell to Japan. As Japan became wealthy, they were putting money into their university system and trying to improve their libraries. Because I was interested in folklore and King Arthur, I decided to do a collection on Arthurian literature and tried to sell it as a collection but ended up doing it as a catalogue, with 1200 books. I had editions of Morte D'Arthur going back to 1634. It was fun to do, I enjoyed that.*

*We're lucky that York has got a mix of people and we're not just dependent on tourists. The average business boomed between 1997 and 2001, for a lot of bookshops in tourist towns. Takings peaked and then went down after 9/11. First of all the Japanese stopped coming over, and after 9/11 American tourists stopped coming. Not just because of the fear of coming over but also they were beginning to realise they could buy on the internet. I started at a good time because there were still lots of country house sales. Sotheby's and Christie's*

Evening Press announced that Neville was to launch the Stonegate Press, a new publishing house, run from Godfrey's. The company published two books, the 'History of Helmsley' and 'Thurston, Archbishop of York 1114-1140'. Two years later the firm won the contract to run a bookshop from the new university at Heslington, within the library buildings. But in June 1968, the shop called Neville Duffield Ltd was sold, along with the university bookshop, to University Bookshops (Oxford) Ltd and a Polish man, Jan Janiurek, came to manage the firm.

Godfrey's Bookshop *(Martin Boyd)*

Sidney Clark recalls his time there:

*I started in 1939 and stayed until June 1958 and went into new bookselling and publishing and from April 1973 I ran James Miles Antiquarian Bookshop in Leeds until retirement. In all I spent 60 years in the book trade.*

*When I joined the firm in April 1939 it had 14 rooms, plus a large attic and shelves on landings and stair walls crammed with books. I well remember the walk to work from Hull Road to Stonegate. The shop bell clanged as I opened the door and I entered a new world. That unmistakeable aroma, the smell of centuries-old leather, paper and ink, mixed with the dust of years, and an indescribable sense that each of the books carried part of the soul of the owners who treasured and loved their books.*

*Willie Fairclough showed me to the office where I was introduced to A
M Harris. Willie then took me on a tour of the shop. There were rare
antiquarian items, private press books, and other collectors' items, old
maps in chests of drawers and cupboards full of engravings. We must
have had over five thousand different prints. Then art, architecture,
children's books, natural history, science, heraldry, family history,*

*Godfreys staff, June 1986; Manager Charles Carey front right, Lizzie
Crabtree second from left at back.* (Elizabeth Crabtree)

*genealogy, literature, drama, poetry, philology. On the next floor politics and law, foreign travel, Yorkshire and English topography, theology, history. Then runs of journals on all subjects.*

*The daily routine was spraying the pavement, washing the plate glass windows, emptying buckets and dusting the downstairs cases and tables and once a week washing the tiled floor in the office. Early lessons in packing parcels were painful. Do it wrongly and the edge of a steel ruler was brought down hard across the knuckles. That first year was spent learning the basic rules of the trade. How to clean, minor repairs and wax polishing leather of all types and ages. The difference between calf, roan, morocco, Niger morocco, Russia, shagreen, lambskin. Also styles of binding and gold tooling. How to clean old maps and prints and the differences between woodcut, wood engraving, copperplate engraving, acid etchings, mezzotints and lithographs.*

*Clearing the unsold stock from a catalogue to the various rooms, made one read the catalogue slip in order to put it in the right room. This taught one how to describe a book, identify its binding, and its size. I still have a measuring stick of 21 more or less standard sizes. As well as learning the different leathers there were different book cloths to identify on books of the Victorian era and later. Over 30 different patterns were used. You also learned the very important art of pricing a book.*

*As the years went by my work on books, cataloguing, going to auctions, buying, increased until I was the second in command. We produced four to six catalogues a year as well as a number of dupli-cated specialist lists, depending on what stock was available.*

*I was there throughout the war. My eyesight was not of the best and I failed the forces medical. I was a handyman. It was a case of, "Can Sidney mend a fuse?", " Can Sidney put me a new spring in the door lock?", and this sort of thing. Particularly for the glass shop next door, Cissy Gordon. Her electricity fused regularly. At the time I was the only active male in the street, apart from two older gentlemen who had shops there. You just helped one another out.*

*Jonathan Palmer and Jan Janiurek at the opening of Godfrey's University Bookshop*
(Blackwell's)

*We bought at sales. We cleared stately homes. We went to one where the butler took us upstairs to the top floor and said, "All these books have to go". And all of the top floor of the house was waist deep in books. Through the centuries, as each new lady of the house took over, she took, out of the library, the books her predecessor had left, wrapped them in newspapers and stacked them in the attic so she had room for her latest novels. And we cleared two furniture pantechnicons out of that one house.*

*We were called in very often particularly with large houses, when the last of the line dies and there's a large library to move.*

*We were the only shop in York until Ken Spelman set up after the war. People would bring in odd items and if they were any good we purchased. An old man came in one day with a bundle of letters, "Are these of any interest?" They were letters from George Stephenson to*

the shop, we'd call at Richardson's the bakers on the corner, which sold beautiful bread, buns and cakes and miniature Hovis loaves.

Most of the staff were graduates and had a real love of books and so the conversations were always interesting. One of my colleagues, Jenny Jones, became a writer of science fantasy books. She, like several others, had studied English at York University.

Jan was quite a character. He had been in the air force and had escaped to England during the Second World War. He had a strong Catholic faith and 1978 was the year of three popes, so Jan's conversation seemed to be dominated by this and he was absolutely thrilled when the Polish Pope John Paul II was elected. Jan was very changeable and sometimes he would be very angry about something and would come up the stairs and bawl one of us out, and then the next day, the door would open and he would come in and sing the Polish national anthem, kneel down and kiss your hand.

I left the company in early 1980, two years before it moved across the road to new premises at 32 Stonegate where the two shops and offices could all be in one building. The advertisement described the shop as having 'tiny passages, small rooms and winding staircases reminiscent of Tolkien's Hobbit, creating an atmosphere that attracts academics and browsers'. At the end of 1985, Jan Janiurek, now 65, retired and was succeeded by Carole Traunter, sent from Blackwell's.

In August 1986 the local press reported that after 80 years of trading, Godfrey's was to become Blackwell's, and would be repainted in blue and gold livery to display the Blackwell name.

Lizzie recalls,

*When we moved over the road, it was much bigger. It was really rather nice with much more useful space. The office was better. But all*

*Blackwell's wanted was to know about the financial aspect. Jan may have been a difficult man but he was a very dedicated bookseller, for which I admired him. He knew about books and bookselling. Part of bookselling is knowing about books. There were a lot of well educated people there who it was good to talk to. Jan's sort of person was going. He was worthy of respect, he was good at what he did, very knowledgeable and very passionately involved in it. It was the death of that bookshop when he went.*

### SPCK Bookshop

SPCK (Society for Propagating Christian Knowledge) was founded nationally in 1698. Within a few years, there were shops all over the country. In 1839 a more formal link was established when Queen Victoria agreed to become patron of the society, a role which has been continued by each successive monarch. The York bookshop opened at 52 Stonegate in the early 1950s where it stayed for 30 years before moving to Goodramgate.

### The Bible Depot

Edith Goreham was born in October 1895. After leaving school, she went into service and then her employer paid for her to study at Redcliffe Bible College, and at the age of 21 she became a colporter selling Bibles door to door. In 1932 she fell in love with and married William Clarke in Rufforth near York and in the 1950s they opened the Bible Depot at 43 Stonegate. Her husband died in August 1964 and she continued to run the business on her own. In September 1969, the Yorkshire Evening Press reported how she escaped uninjured when the upstairs ceiling of her shop collapsed. Beryl Burkett recalls meeting Mrs Clarke at St Andrew's Gospel Hall.

*Mrs Clarke and friend at the Bible Depot* (Martin Boyd)

*And going to Mrs Clarke's as a family to tea on Sunday afternoons, all six of us. They never had children but she liked young people. Mrs Clarke had a friend who was a farmer and I remember getting our little dog from her, Judy, she was a terrier.*

Beryl's sister, Carole Spreadbury, also recalls,

*When I was young, my father would take me into her shop where I would sit enthralled, as she related in her own unique way, which usually included putting her hand on your arm to emphasise a point, her faith or some particular incident in her life. People saw her as a pillar of strength and a wise counsellor.*

*View of Stonegate with the Bible Depot on the left at No. 43. (Martin Boyd)*

She had a connection with Rev David Watson of St Michael le Belfrey, and shortly before his death, he wrote of her, 'She was an enormous encourager for us as a congregation and without her prayers and incredible help in those vital early days, the work at St Cuthbert's and then St Michael's would probably never have started'.

During the 1960s and '70s, Mrs Clarke held meetings in her home, which was above the shop. She welcomed young people and university students to share her hospitality. Many York people remember her with fondness. She was also quite eccentric, as Jill Murray recalls.

*She had this amazing little Bible shop. She'd been married to a sea captain, a commander. She was an absolute character. She used to come to our shop sometimes and was often in her dressing gown and slippers. She was an incredible old lady.*

Gill Douglas recalls visiting the shop.

*I only met her once. And I loved it in there. And on the door it had a little piece of paper, four inches by five which just said 'Under Divine Protection'. I just walked in one day and I said, "I'm Gill, I live in the lighthouse and I've heard about you", and within five minutes she had me in the kitchen in the back.*

*She was a very sweet lady who took a real interest in individuals and had a good memory for anyone who had been into her shop.*

In the early 1980s, Edith Clarke moved into a nursing home in Norton where she died in 1985 at the age of 90.

## *The Printers*

### *James Hare/ Bullivant's*

James Hare established a printing works in the 1870s at 5 Stonegate, next to the Punch Bowl Inn. He died in November 1886 at the age of 43, but his son took over. By the time the younger James died in March 1928, at the age of 63, they had been trading for 50 years. The business continued under the same name, being run by Harold Goodson. John Bullivant's father took over the firm when

*he came to York in 1959. He'd  always been fascinated with printing and thought it was an area of industry that would never die out. Little*

*Bullivant's Printing Works (John Bullivant)*

*did he know! They looked at places in Northallerton, they even went to Herne Bay in Kent but they chose the one in Stonegate. He bought the business and Harold carried on working for my father, for three or four years. I started in 1962 and we changed it to J W Bullivant and Son in 1968.*

*It was run down. There was no quality. Harold did the bits of paper-work and walked round the town with deliveries and things and liaised with the existing customers as they came in and introduced them to my father. There was the feeling that there was a lot of potential there.*

*It was on two floors. Downstairs there was a Payne and Sons diamond guillotine. There was a Double Demi Wharfedale, a Quad Crown Wharfedale, a folding machine. It was all driven by a five horsepower motor with counter shafting and several belts driven from one central motor. Upstairs were all the typefaces, the frames for the compositors. There'd be half a dozen right the way down one side. There was an old hoist for large frames, pages of type for the big presses downstairs.*

*There was a Heidelburg platen and an Arab platen. The sheet of paper is effectively laid onto a flat plate, as opposed to being rolled round the cylinder onto the type which would be a cylinder press. The cylinder presses were Quad Crown, 20 by 30 inches, or 30 by 40. I remember doing posters on them for the York Festival. We do know that Hare used that Quad machine for printing books.*

*It was a family business. The customers were mostly businesses. My mother would go in and do the finishing. Packing, folding, collating, putting various duplicate books together. People didn't have computers, everything was hand done with carbon paper. We only got litho when we moved to Bishopthorpe Road in 1972, which is simply to get away from the parking problems.*

*I remember getting paper and carting it up the passage. Three and a half tons of paper came on an articulated lorry from Scotland. I stacked it in Stonegate, and barrowed it up the passage into the down-stairs area.*

*Before my dad bought the business, he was fiddling about with it. He'd got some kit at home and I'd played with it. And I found I could set type, at eight and a half years old. I realised I could use my hands. I decided that craft was going to be the thing with me rather than academia. And unlike some father son relationships, I got on well with him. We might have had a disagreement but we never had a fight.*

*You'd stand for hours at a type setting frame which holds various styles and sizes of type. You pick the size case out and style that you want, and you spent hours picking letters out individually and putting them into a type setting stick, left to right, upside down, and making sure every line is exactly the same length. If you have an accident, they'd call it a 'printer's pie'. The printer's devil depicts the apprentice who hasn't learnt to be careful and drops his first case of type and what he's got to do then is sort the whole pile out and put it back in the case. We've all done it.*

*'Printer's devil' in Stonegate*

(Lesley Collett)

*A good compositor can do 1000 characters an hour. Say there's 2000 characters on a page, it's a long job. We used to get the plates made at York Graphic Arts.*

*We did pretty much black and white. The difficulty with printing letter press is that the letters are individual, and it not being a perfect science, occasionally they came loose. And in the Holmes vertical, the letters sometimes popped out. And while I was looking at this, I*

*John (Jack), Amy, Barbara and John Bullivant junior at family wedding, 1957 (John Bullivant)*

*noticed that the heading said, 'Ladies' loves', and it should have said, 'Ladies' gloves'. So we had to put the sheets back through again and put the G in.*

*The Holmes vertical had a wet spray. That was messy 'cos it used to get in the air and it'd make everything sticky eventually.*

*We used to do work for Yorkshire Insurance. As happened to a lot of printers, the bigger customers put their own print plant in, in-house printing on small litho presses. But in those days there were lots of printers, Noel Richardson in Little Stonegate, in Grape Lane a one man band H E Downdes. Rusholme's in High Ousegate. Morley's in Petergate, Coward's in Peasholme Green, Cobham Smith in Barker Lane. Sellington's, Cansfield's, Thomas Dick. There was a lot of work.*

*Rusholme's had a bookbinder called Tommy Duck and the few books that we needed binding properly were done by him. We printed the day bills for the Theatre Royal. One winter, the chap from the theatre came round in expectation that they would be ready but we hadn't got them back from Rusholme's. So Harold Godson said, "They're round at our poster department, I'll just go and fetch them", and he toddled off round to pick them up. Bear in mind it was a winter's day and it was cold. The upstairs of the place was heated by two coke stoves*

John Bullivant *(Mike Race)*

*which would be fired up, particularly on a Monday morning, and they used to fill the place with smoke. You couldn't see from one end of the room to the other. My father would often send me out for a walk in town while the smoke cleared. While Harold Goodson was at the 'poster department', this chap was warming himself in front of this fire, looking at a naughty calendar on the wall behind him. And he got so close to the stove, that he scorched his coat. What he told his wife when he got home, I don't know.*

*We started doing programmes for the York Light Opera Society. I think the first one was 'Orpheus in the Underworld'. So we were doing four A5 pages at a time, you can't do a lot on a Heidelburg platen. As business built up we wanted something that was more efficient to expand our repertoire. We had a Miehle vertical first, then that broke down, so we swapped it.*

*My dad used to record the sales alphabetically. If they were frequent customers they'd have their own page in what he called the Family Bible, the family being all the customers. When I retired in 2006, we still had one of the original customers from the very early days. J H Wright, the coal merchant. We'd print coal delivery books. We got our printing inks from Richardson's Printing Company at Rowlands Gill, County Durham and paper from Spicer's, Wiggins Teape and three and a half tons came from Scotland. The printing inks all smell differently. Manufacturers have different smells. The Richardson company rep came round with some additive to thin the ink down; I took the lid off, and I thought, 'Euthymol toothpaste'.*

*I remember them talking about Wonder White Wove at one shilling and an eighth of a penny a pound. It was large post, foolscap, double foolscap, foolscap folio. And there were silly sizes like Double Elephant. Quarto (10 by 8 which is effectively A4), large post which is 16½ by 21.*

*We used to do a bit of work for Jackson's Signs and Noel Wainhouse Electricians in Coffee Yard. A chap called Mr Ledward of Jackson's Signs. When he came in for a job, he was there for an hour, he knew everything that everybody else didn't know. Working life in those days was a lot more leisurely. I suppose with a family business if you didn't get done what you needed to get done by teatime, you'd go back on a night and finish it off. So it was a different era.*

*Life was very simple. They'd know what they wanted. They often brought a card in from somewhere and said, "I want something like this". Then we would perhaps show them the Stephenson Blake Book of Typefaces.*

*When litho came in, it made printing a lot quicker. Whereas letter press is a mechanical system, litho's a chemical system. It relies on the interaction between water and oil and you've got to get the balance right. It was starting to get technical then. The inks changed, the system changed. Technology started with litho which prompted photo type setting which eventually prompted computers and then software. Now they're doing it all digitally.*

*We did a book for a doctor who lived in the Leyburn area. It was a tribute to a friend of theirs, it was poems of Coverdale. We got Rush-olme's to bind that in green suede with the name embossed in gold on the cover. That was done at Stonegate with green and gold illuminated initials for each first letter.*

*I'm sad to see craftsmanship go. When I'm out at craft fairs, if I see somebody do wood turning the old way with a couple of trestles, and a foot treddle and a bow and a string, that's fascinating. Because skills are going out. Technology is taking over. Latterly we had machinery which was quite complicated, it was all a matter of timing. The timing of the suction, the timing of the grippers getting hold of the sheet and then the suckers releasing the suction. But the machinery was rela-tively simple and you could repair it yourself. With modern printing machines, you can't repair, you get a technician in from somewhere.*

## Noel Richardson's

The only other more recent printer in the area was Noel Richardson who ran his business in Little Stonegate. The property had once been the Ebenezer Chapel. He took over the company from Coultas and Vollans in 1946 and changed the name to Noel Richardson in January 1958. His son, Linden Richardson, was appointed director in 1975. Noel's wife Mary died in 1988 and Noel died the following year in April 1999 aged 89. In the same year the business closed, and

*Banks Edition, the collections of piano music. I think that started in the 1880s, the publishing side, and it went on until the early 1970s when Peter Banks retired and sold it to Margaret and Ramsay Silver and they still continue to own it to this day as Banks Music Publications. It was well patronised by composers. Once you established an identity for publishing good choral music, composers and arrangers would come to you, "Could you publish this for me?" Some would sell very well and some not so well. Mr Banks had a panel of readers, mainly composers, to select works for publication. Thousands of manuscripts were submitted annually.*

*Miss Banks was involved with Dame Fanny Waterman who runs the Leeds International Piano Competition in Leeds Town Hall and also one or two musical festivals. It perpetuated the name of Banks and brought it to a wider audience. I remember in about 1978, a big national conference of organists in St John's College. At the end there was a dinner for the delegates and local VIPs. Miss Banks said, "Malcolm would you come with me?" This was a rare occasion 'cos she was always working, she never had an evening off. She had her last holiday in 1937. We were escorted into the dining room and about 50 to 100 delegates stood up immediately, and she said, "What do we do, Malcolm?" "Keep walking, Miss Banks, keep walking". It was a great occasion, and I was so fortunate to be there and have Janet Marie Banks on my arm.*

*People had great affection for her. I went into the general office one Saturday with a piece of music I wanted to buy and she was asleep, her head cradled in her right arm. I was just about to creep out and this roused her. I gingerly said, "Could I buy this piece of music? It's the Lamentation by Sir Edward Bairstow from York Minster". "Oh take it with my compliments". She was very kind hearted and generous.*

*I'd go out in the van with Derek Cryer, the brass band and wind band manager, to displays and competitions to Bellevue, Manchester.*

*We'd take a van of music for the weekend. In November there was
the national brass band finals in the Albert Hall. That was a real
treat. We'd have a meal out in London and stay on the stall all day
Saturday. It expanded as trade grew. We'd go Connor's Quay in
North Wales and once up to Loch Gellig north of Edinburgh.*

*Mail order customers would include schools and colleges and bands,
individual piano teachers and individual customers, and in September,
we would be busy with schools sending orders in, and towards
Christmas it was busy with carols and choral music. We'd get orders
from abroad too. At the shop I had a call from Beijing and we've had
calls from Australia for music. People move away and take our name
with them as a good source of music. Our name goes before us. A
typical day's postbag would contain orders for 'Teddy Bear's Picnic',
'Blue Danube', 'Schumann Piano Concerto', and Chopin's 'Etude and
Nocturnes'. We had many requests for works by Dr Tertius Noble,
one time organist at the Minster and personal friend of Cecil Banks.
We had a very big textbook department. In 1982, Stanley Sadie was
editor of the new Grove Dictionary of Music, it was 20 volumes and
about £800, and we were invited to the launch at the Viking Hotel for
Yorkshire. When it was the York Early Music Festival, my colleague
Nicholas King would take a display of music, or when Dame Janet
Baker was coming to the university.*

*Nicholas and Ken [Stabler] would do the window display. When it was
Miss Banks's birthday, somebody would put a bouquet in the window.
I remember when it was the Prince of Wales's wedding, we had the
first copy of the anthem, 'Let the people praise thee O God', by William
Matthias. We were fortunate because it was published by Oxford
University Press and the northern rep lived in York so he brought us
a special copy and we put it in the window. At the time it was a best
seller. Or if it was the Proms in London, we'd put the programme and
LP covers in the window. On Stonegate corner was the organ window
and the window down Stonegate was the instrument window.*

142

years later in 1994, Richard Barry Junior, by then a well-known figure and alderman in Hull, visited 41 Stonegate when it was once more on the market. He recalled being evacuated from Hull during the war to stay with his aunt and grandmother in the flat on the fifth floor above the business. He described,

> *The ornate staircase with wrought iron Tudor rose and vine balustrades, which echoes the design of the grand ones to be found at the Royal Station Hotel. It was here I used to fling paper darts down the staircase well. And I would spit down there, hoping to hit the staff parking their bikes in the basement.*

Sheila Pinch was born in 1933 and started work with the company in 1947.

> *I'd set my heart on children's nursing but was too late to get on the list. A neighbour said that Swallow and Barry wanted an apprentice so I went and had an interview. Miss Barry was impressed I didn't bring my mother or father with me. We had to pay a premium, and had five years apprenticeship, and it was well worth it. The place had a name as a most exclusive shop. I had a wonderful time until I left when I had my baby daughter who is now 50. I remember Dr Crane, the Medical Officer of Health, she was one of my customers. [The first female in this role in Britain]. Miss Barry was a very kind person. I got on extremely well with her.*

> *The décor was a natural colour, it was dark cream. There was a staircase with a wooden rail and at the bottom was a circle where Miss Barry used to put fresh flowers in a glass bowl. They looked gorgeous. In the salon at the top of the stairs, you turned right to two cubicles. There was a settee in the salon with a little table with all the best magazines like the Tatler.*

> *When you went in the shop there was a big glass cabinet with special*

*perfumes, a lovely olde worlde coal fire and a nice chair in reception. There was a lovely tearoom there, and the towels were laundered in the basement by cleaners, with an old fashioned mangle. Mr Barry and Miss Barry made their own products, used oils to make dressaline, it had the Swallow and Barry label on it. We always had perfumes, that was Miss Barry's side, she didn't do hairdressing. She was in charge of wages and the shop. She had a flat on the top floor. They made their own wigs, for the National Health, not privately. They could bring the wig back every three months to be redressed. We were the only ones to do this. We'd put it onto a model head and clean it.*

*Mr Raines was in the gent's salon. They got the chance to have a salon in the Station Hotel and he moved there. He was very precise, and very good with the nobility. My treat on Friday was to take his wage packet and bring the takings back. You could walk about York with money in your bag then.*

*Mr Barry came back from the war with a wounded arm, he was never 100% but he managed to work. The beautician Dolores did facials and nails. She was there about six to eight years, and they never replaced her. I did part hairdressing and part behind the counter. Katherine Worsley came in regularly, with two poodles which Miss Barry would look after. She would buy some things on her own account and things to order for the bathroom for visitors, such as bath oils, were on Daddy's account. She was a lovely person. Lord Deramore and his wife were good customers. They lived at Heslington Hall.*

*Nancy Lockwood worked there and she and I used to go to the Art Gallery in Leeds for tuition and there was a dance one time and she did my hair. I went to Homburger's in Leeds and got a Russian outfit. Nancy was born at Long Marston and we'd go there and stay the night at her aunt's for parties and dances. She went off to be a hair-dresser on her own in Fishergate. I remember Princess Alexandra coming to Stonegate. My Dad was on York City Council and was*

*Princess Alexandra visits York, 1950s* (Yorkshire Evening Press)

*Sheriff. The Mayor walked with the Princess and my Dad walked behind with her lady in waiting. He smiled and waved at me. Apparently he said, "I am as proud of her as the Duke would have been of his daughter if he'd been here today".*

*I left in 1959. I used to go in to see Miss Barry regularly with the baby and she gave me a beautiful hairbrush and clothes brush with backing in pale pink.*

151

The staff at the shop were told the story of a ghost in the premises.

*A little girl, Flossy, the daughter of a doctor who lived there in Victorian times. She was having a birthday party, probably the top floor would have been the bedrooms and fell over the stairs and landed in the basement. Miss Barry used to say she felt a presence. She said the girl walked through doors, she was Victorian in a crinoline dress.* [Records show that the house was built in 1865 for a York surgeon on the site of the White Horse Inn].

Angela Fenton became an apprentice at the beginning of 1950.

*I was 15, and I got £1 a week, then after six months it was 22/6d and after a year it was 25s. I had to fold towels, collect towels, iron towels, and run round the corner to the café with a little silver coffeepot to get six pennyworth of coffee. And she'd say, "Come on, comb us up". So every time I went there, I'd to go through the back and comb her up.*

*I'd watch Mr Barry do a hair colour, sweep up the bits, fill up the shampoo bottles and the conditioning cream. There were two juniors and 11 seniors. We had to look after all of those, shampooing for them and running around after them. They made your life hell. We'd clean the wigs in petrol, swing them round outside in the back yard and peg them on the line. Then set them and put them in this massive gas oven downstairs to dry. We'd to stay in the evening to learn hairdressing 'cos during the day we were so busy doing all these chores. There were five floors altogether. The basement where the coke place was and at the bottom of the stairs a little place where they put their bikes. There was a corridor and all little rooms and a chemical cupboard, then a big open area with a work table where we did all the wigs and everything. Then a little room where the gas oven was and a sink. The men from the gents' salon used to have a couple of days each to go down and keep the stove going for hot water. Up the back stairs was a staff room and a laundry room, with a great big old ringer, it was horren-*

*dous. Then it brought you onto the floor of hairdressing with the blocks of cubicles. Mr Barry made his own shampoo out of green soft soap, in this big barrel. He'd melt it down on the gas ring and stood over it stirring it, hubble bubble toil and trouble. And then made the conditioning cream in an enamel bowl, putting oil of verbena in for a lemony smell.*

*There were seats at the top of the stairs for people waiting and Mr Barry's cubicles were at the front. You had to bool the dryers in and pull the curtain across. They all thought nobody would hear when they were in there but there was a gap at the top and you'd to be careful who was talking to whom. It was hard work pulling those dryers and trolleys around. We'd no rollers then, it was all finger waves and pincurls. And the Macdonald machine. Mr Barry did a Macdonald perm, he used to get about three a year. It would take days to get this box ready 'cos there was red and white strings, and blue and white strings and they had little buckets on this big round machine hanging down, all with numbers on, and this spiral winder, and they had to be fitted on number by number. It took about six hours. His arm was very flat and scarred, he couldn't do shampoos and sets when he came back from the war. We'd help him with his perms. I think of him walking up the corridor to warn you he was coming, and tapping his comb on the wall.*

*But it was where you got the best training. After you'd done your apprenticeship and two years as improver, that enabled you to leave if you wanted to but you daren't at that time. The theatre people would come on a Monday morning and if it was a period play, I would go at night to comb up at the theatre. I remember Barry Prendergast. [The York composer John Barry]. He was at St Peter's School when he would come. I used to practise shampooing on him. I used to set Miss Barry's hair, but she'd go to London to get it permed.*

*When I started they hadn't an overall that fit me, it was a great big*

*wide thing down to the floor, we had grey overalls with a blue collar
and top pockets piped with big cuffs. And I'd to wrap it round.*

Angela's father, Fred Fenton, was a hairdresser with a business in
Bootham.

*My mother wanted me to go to Prime's secretarial school in Priory
Street. But I wanted to be a hairdresser. From being three I'd sit in my
high chair in the salon and watch him and all I ever wanted to do was
cut hair. I used to trim anything when I was a kid. You know those big
old chenille tablecloths with long fringes, I'd get under this big table
and I'd snip all these things.*

*I had to do exams. Mr Barry told me, "I'll send you to L'Oreal school
for two weeks, but you've got to promise me that when you come
back, you won't leave, when I've paid for you to go". And my mum
went with me and we stayed in Russell Square. I had to get the bus at
Euston station every morning, it was off Oxford Street. Mrs Gaitskell
[wife of the Prime Minister] would come to get her hair set 'cos the
girl who used to teach us had worked at Steiner's.*

*It went from finger wave setting to rollers in the '50s. They'd just have
five at the front in that Gina Lollobrigida Italian style. It was £3. 15s
for a Wella wireless perm and three guineas for a Jamil perm, it was a
machineless perm with vapits. You'd dip them in water and put them
on. Then plastic rollers came in and Marcel waves went. And Bombash
curling where you had to section off about an inch square and then roll
that round into a curl with the iron which was on a gas burner. You had
to test that on paper so you didn't singe the hair. When you got near the
back you had to put a comb underneath so it didn't burn the neck. They
wouldn't allow it now, it was dangerous really.*

If the hairdressers wanted to do each other's hair, they had to ask
permission, and do it after work.

*I remember Lundy, she would never ask. She worked in what Miss Barry called naughty corner, at the bottom end of the corridor. I was once shampooing her hair in that little cubicle and he's coming down the corridor, so I'm rubbing it harder and harder. She said, "What the hell are you doing? It's too hard". He came and stood right at the side of the bowl. I brought her up, and she said, "Oh can I have my hair done?" I was terrified. I'd said, "Have you asked him?" "No, he'll never know, come on, get it done".*

Gadsby's art shop in Petergate had its rear entrance facing the rear of Swallow and Barry. Angela recalls,

*Jean Gadsby used to sing and Frankie Vaughan was a friend of theirs. He would visit and sing out of the bathroom window, that song 'Green Door'.*

Sue Taylor started her apprenticeship in 1955, and worked there until 1961.

*I was at college in York and I'd been doing shorthand and typing for two years and didn't want to work in an office. I wanted to be a hairdresser. I went and asked Mr Barry and he said, "I've just taken on two apprentices last year". He thought I was too old 'cos I was 17 but I wouldn't take no for an answer and I just went in every lunchtime until he did. He was a wonderful cutter and he was a trichologist. One of only a few in the country. He was concentrating on the condition of hair.* [Today the Institute of Trichologists has 119 members in the whole of the UK. They are specially trained in hair and scalp disorders, hair growth, and professional wigmaking.]

*There were three other men when I started, Arthur Eades, Clarry Rains and Derek Lee, in the gents' department. We'd go to Leeds for training on a Monday night and we had to get all our jobs done before we went. Heather [Norton] and I went to Scarborough to do*

155

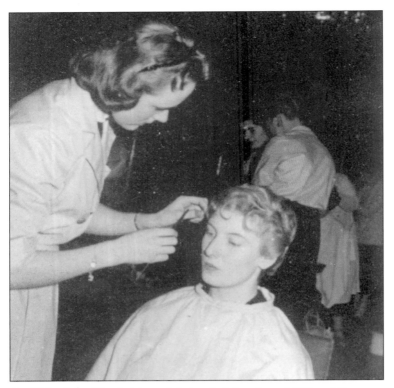

*Sue Kirby doing Wendy Morton's hair at hairdressing exhibition at the
York Assembly Rooms, c. 1956* (Neville England)

*the hairdressing registration examination. And we had to go on a
Sunday 'cos it was the only day that the salon wasn't in use. We had
to take our own models and had to do everything - perming, cutting,
Marcel waving, shampooing, setting, colouring. I remember the brush
wave when that came out. I thought it was lovely. It was very gentle
and it didn't last long. For the Jamil perm, you put a sort of clamp
on the hair, and you wound it in. It fizzed and steamed, it sparked
and crackled and there was an ozone smell to it. You had to be very
careful, and watch out for people's scalps. Then there was the Lockwell
system. Little tiny rollers with tiny hooks, very effective but very time*

*consuming. I remember borrowing it when I was going to a wedding. He wasn't keen if you got married. And you still had to keep your old name, you couldn't be Mrs So-and-So.*

Once the hairdressers were fully qualified, they got commission. They had to take a minimum of £25 and then would get commission of one shilling in the pound. They had to buy a notebook and work it out, and hand the books in on Friday nights.

Sue also recalls one of the romances that existed.

*I remember Pauline, the receptionist. She was a lovely girl and was going out with a chap who worked in Nigeria. He'd talked about getting engaged next time he got back. But she never heard from him. It had been two or three years, so she was going out with someone else, and then he came back. He just thought she would be waiting. He said, "Will you meet me for lunch?", in the Chinese restaurant in Stonegate. He said, "I want to marry you", and he talked her round, and they got engaged and flew off to Nigeria and it was so romantic. But it was sad because eventually she died young of cancer.*

Zoe Hutchinson did not train at Swallow and Barry, but was already qualified when she started work there in 1953.

*I had very good training, five years in Malton. I wanted to widen my outlook so I went for an interview with Mr Barry. He hired me on the spot, I was an expert cutter but I used to do it quite differently to what he used to teach. Then I went down to London and did the tinting and perming qualification.*

*I got 6 guineas a week when I got married. I had a customer who was a squadron leader's wife and she got me this flat in Marygate. We got good tips and it would buy something for the meal at night. I would shop on the way home in Bootham.*

*We had a lot of loyalty towards Mr Barry 'cos it was a nice place to work. When I think of him, it's of him twiddling with the Marcel wave tongs, he used to heat them in the gas flame. Hairdressers nowadays wouldn't be able to do all the finger waves and pincurls.*

The staff would go to the annual Hairdressers' Ball in the Assembly Rooms. It was held in the winter and was open to anyone who worked for a hairdresser, and their partners.

*Hairdressers' Ball, Assembly Rooms, 1958.*
*Left to right: Sue Kirby, Jean and Danny Browne, Ray Norton and Heather Page*
(Neville England)

Heather Norton also worked there in the 1950s.

*You trained all the time but there were firms that wanted to update you, with the colours that were coming in. I remember Mr Barry said, "I'm going to try this colour on you". It was somewhere between orange and red, a hideous colour. I went home and my mother said, "Out, you're like a street girl". I don't even know the make, but it was*

158

## Chapter 8

# *The Churches*

The Church of St Helen's once fronted onto Stonegate, with its church-yard extending into what is now St Helen's Square. The plan of the church is medieval, and the original building was made of wood, but most of the church has been rebuilt at some time or other. It is broadly 15th century in style, the oldest object being the 12th century font. The Reformation led to the sale and partial demolition of the church though an Act reinstated it in 1553 because of local protesters who said its suppression had 'defaced and deformed the city'. The old graveyard became the square in 1733 and the bones were taken out and moved to a small space on the south west side of Davygate. Blake Street was also widened so that carriages and coaches could attend the Mansion House and the Assembly Rooms, in Georgian York.

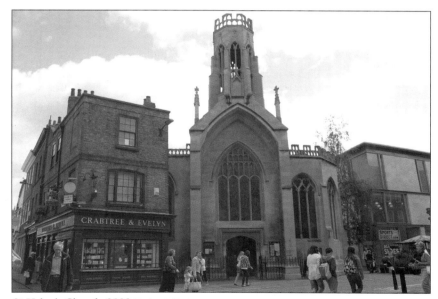

*St Helen's Church, 2009 (Lesley Collett)*

*St Helen's Square before widening, c. 1905 (Christine Lancaster)*

The church is named after Helena, the mother of Constantine, who was proclaimed Emperor in York in 306. She is widely revered in both Orthodox and Catholic Europe, and particularly in York in the Middle Ages. She is said to have visited the Holy Land, recovered relics of the True Cross and to have founded churches in Bethlehem and on the Mount of Olives. The year after Constantine legalised Christianity within the Roman Empire, York was one of only two cities from Britain to send a bishop to the Council of Arles. The existence of a church dedicated to St Helen within the ancient Roman fortress is a reminder of this pivotal era in the history of the church in York. Significant remains of Roman buildings almost certainly lie beneath the church.

The church contained a large amount of decorated glass, of which the only remainder is the west window which contains glass from the 14th, 15th and 16th centuries.

*for 20 years until four or five years ago. You are responsible for the building. Repairs and that sort of thing, and you've got to look after the money, to make sure that you pay the bills. It's a very responsible job. During the week you're arranging for builders, opening the church and locking it up at night, and looking after visitors. I was also a sacristan, looking after the altar linen.*

*The church has been redundant, in the Middle Ages and then in eighteen something, and it's always come to life again. The church-wardens have to do quite a lot of work, because you've got to arrange for clergy to take Sunday services. There are always plenty of spare retired clergy around in York. They are very helpful, and they like taking services.*

*On Christmas Eve we had a midnight mass. And that was the only time we really had problems. There'd be banging on the doors, and St Helen's Square really became very unpleasant. A lot of our people used to get their cars damaged. Like a lot of city-centre churches, we just stopped having midnight mass.*

*We've had lunchtime concerts for quite a long time. A lot of the American choirs came to York and they used St Helen's for their concerts. We have quite a lot of organ recitals. And they're very attractive. The Archbishop's been using St Helen's launching that appeal for Zimbabwe.*

*There's a Chinese group, I think they're mostly students from the University. And they wanted their own service in Mandarin. So the vicar of St Michael-le-Belfrey asked if they could use St Helen's. I don't know what their service is like. It won't be a Eucharist, that's for sure, they won't have incense, I think there's a lot of music groups.*

The other local Anglican church, St Michael le Belfrey, is famous for its connection with Guy Fawkes who was baptised there in

1570, having been born at the rear of 23 High Petergate opposite St Michael's (although there are some who question this, and believe he was actually born in Stonegate). The Fawkes family was well-known in York, with ancestors who had been Sheriffs and Lord Mayors. The church was rebuilt between 1525 and 1537, during King Henry VIII's break with Rome. It has always been the largest parish church in the city, originally serving a wealthy community of merchants and craftsmen. In the late 18th century the vicar William Richardson was known for his powerful preaching. A large gallery was built as the congregation expanded. He also founded the York Sunday Schools Committee, visited the poor and cared for prisoners, becoming known as the 'Father of the York clergy'. In the 1960s the congregation had dwindled down to a handful of people and there was talk of closure. Another gifted preacher, David Watson, came from St Cuthbert's to St

*Archbishop of York Dr John Sentamu plays drums outside St Michael le Belfrey with members of the congregation, 2007 (Gill Douglas)*

*a massive coronary thrombosis and ended up in the County Hospital.
I knew David ten years before we got married. When I came to York I
was 21, he was still a teenager and you didn't set your sights on somebody in their teens. Later on we did work together quite a bit in church
and then we realised we were in love and got married in 1967 in
Elim, and then my daughter was married in Elim church and David's
brother and sisters got married there. It was a special place for us.*

*It used to be a billiard hall before Elim took it. There were leatherette
tip up seats. We've known times when they were sitting on the floor
and the stairs and window ledges. Most nights there were meetings,
which wouldn't work now. There wasn't TV and the things younger
people go to.* [In the 1970s, Dorothy worked with the Tang Hall
Sunday School as pianist, secretary and treasurer. She was also
involved in the music side, singing solos at some of the services

*Wedding of Elizabeth Watson and Martin Rowley, 1989* (David Watson)

including ones to old people's homes and one at Armley Jail
attended by 340 inmates].

*It became difficult when foot streets started and you had to be out of
Swinegate by 12 o'clock. Even weddings and funerals were difficult
'cos you are in the middle of a shopping area and just across the road
was a wholesale greengrocer's and what you didn't want in your
wedding pictures were all these warehouses and vegetables strewn
around. Nothing was very nice down there, the shops weren't very
thrilling. Now they've got these posh shops and it's become upmarket
in Swinegate.*

June Noble was born in 1930 in Acomb.

*My Mum died when I was eight and my sister was five. I stayed a
lot at my Grandma's and my two maiden aunts attended Elim so we
went along. At Sunday School Miss Cookridge had a sand tray and I
remember her telling Bible stories and sticking figures in the tray, like
the 'Lion's Den' and the 'Fiery Furnace'.*

*Towards the end of the war, my auntie was in the ATS, I met a lot of
her friends, some Canadians. Being a central church, people would
come into town. I think we were all one big happy family. My sister
and I had no mum, so we were invited to homes and I seemed to have
lots of people looking out for me. It may have come from the war years
that we all drew together. I remember going to prayer meetings on an
evening, we seemed to do a lot of praying. I think the people who came
in who were away from home were drawn in because of the friendship.
People involved them.*

*I carried on until I was about 17 when I started work at Cooke,
Troughton and Sims. That's where I met my husband. I stopped going
for quite a while, but then I went back when my children were about
ten. On the corner of Grape Lane and Swinegate they had a big indoor*

*car park with a roof, we borrowed it on a Sunday. The other side was warehouses for the market, there was lots of fruit and vegetables there. At the end of the war we kind of felt starved. We would pick up old apples and eat the apple core and everything.*

*They did 'tell-a-tourist' for quite a while, a lot of people went out on the streets, handing out gospels in different languages. Brought people in and we gave them meals. We did have a lot of special meetings, and events where we'd get a big minister in the Elim movement. I remember George Canty and he painted a picture every night, and he would give a message as he painted, like Rolf Harris. Whoever brought the largest amount of people in got it. I remember my husband once got the picture.*

*It was well known because years later people would say, "Are you still going to Elim?" It brought a lot of children in on buses for Sunday School. It did a lot of good work. I'm always meeting people who went to Sunshine Corner.*

*People don't have a foundation now. But other people will say we were brainwashed. We didn't think it was. We really loved it. It was varied, and we had lots of friends. People seemed to be more polite. Children were respectful in the home. In the '50s it started to change because we could get more things. Then materialism came in. It meant wanting more and more. After the war, we were all thinking more of our own little unit. Before we were poor and we soldiered on together. I was young, I didn't see the hard work parents had to do in the home, with meagre rations, cooking for a family, all the washing and sewing. We have so much now, we just press a button.*

## Chapter 9

# *Entertainment*

### *The Dance Academy*

Robert Cowper started his Dance Academy in Peter Lane and moved to Number 8 Stonegate in 1860. Cowper was described as a 'professor of dancing and deportment' in the York directory of 1881. He was also a musician and was one of the first violins in the York Choral Society and bandmaster of the York Artillery Corps. He died in 1885 aged 65 and his son Arthur took over. In the Yorkshire Evening Press of 12th November 1900, he advertised 'Minuets, Gavottes, refined and artistic skirt dances, latest novelties of the ballroom'. He was by then President of the UK Alliance of Professional Teachers of Dancing. In 1913, he added calisthenics and tango classes to the list.

Arthur had three daughters, Gladys, Elsie and Beatrice, and by 1929, he had been joined by them, advertising,

> The Academy for Dancing. Mr and the Misses Cowper. Classes on Mondays and Thursdays at 8pm, children Saturday at 6pm. Lessons on violin and mandolin and private lessons by appointment.

Cowper died in 1937, but his daughters continued, and by 1945, they were holding a 'Ballroom Dancing Practice Class at Feasegate Café', and by 1958 were still offering ballroom dancing tuition from their home on The Mount.

Harry Murray recalls attending the academy in the 1930s.

> *It had a dancehall on the first floor, and a supper room on the ground floor. There was a big mirror at each end which ran from ground to ceiling. The Misses Cowper looked like Hinge and Brackett and wore long scarves, one red, one green.*

194

## The Night Clubs

Just past Hannon's fruit shop, at number 11 Stonegate was a night-club in the early 1960s called The Mandrake which changed in 1965 to the Zarf Club. On 2nd June they announced in the Yorkshire Evening Press,

*"The Missfits*
*York's youngest group with a big following.*
*Admission 1/6d."*

---

**Tel. 22904 ZARF CLUB 11 Stonegate**

**ALL SET AT THE ZARF for lots of fun this Xmas weekend**
**Surprise items—Dancing Competition—new James Bond effects**

## XMAS EVE
## THE ROLL MOVEMENT
Come and dance to the group everyone is raving about.

## SUNDAY. Doors open 4 p.m.
## THE BREAKERS
**After their record-breaking tour with the Everly's, the North's leading Comedy/Beat Group.**

---

*December 1965*

In October 1965, the Pretty Things were due to play there, but they were two hours late arriving as the van with their instruments was in a crash. Local group Gideon's Few who were the support act, played a much longer set and then lent their equipment to the band. Gideon's Few also broke a record by playing there for ten hours non-stop in December of that year.

On October 11th 1967 the club became the Old World. Things tightened up and only members were allowed in. It was well-known for

*The Roll Movement at St Mary's Abbey. Left to right: John Cartwright, Dave Williams, Cliff Wade, Pete Shaw.* (*York Oral History Society*)

its ultra-violet lighting in the basement where live music and dancing took place. Phil Calvert who was a musician, recalls,

> *It was on three levels. It had a coffee lounge on the ground floor but there was a cellar as well, and often jazz in there, all very low lit. When you went upstairs it was all chemin de fer, black jack and roulette. We'd go and watch, certain people went in for that sort of thing and they were always there, with piles of money, used to amaze me. I think when it was the Mandrake we played down there with the Tycoons. We saw some good up and coming bands there. They had the first proper bouncers in York, Mick the Masher Allinson and his brother Spen.*

York jazz musician, Ron Burnett, played regularly at the Old World, being paid £2.10s each, which was quite a lot of money then. He remembers that the band played in the cellar and the fire exits were dodgy, so that a real fire would have been quite a disaster.

Ian Gillis recalls,

*There was a casino, it attracted people that wanted a game of cards or try their hand at roulette or blackjack. I don't remember there being any scandal about loading the tables or people fiddling or anything. I think the legislation came in to stop casinos at a later stage. Before that it was the Zarf Club. I think the song then was 'You've Lost That Loving Feeling', the Righteous Brothers.* [People have mentioned that amphetamines and so-called soft drugs were available at the club.] *In those days we were at the very beginning of the university, in the early 60s. When I was in the police force, the students union were finding their feet somewhat. They'd have marches and it was all LSD, these hallucinogenic drugs.*

*Phil's* [Calvert] *dad was six foot eight. And he was Sergeant 49,* [Drugs and Firearms Officer]. *If he was here today he wouldn't recognise the drugs scene. You knew who was using them because they stood out like a sore thumb, whereas today it's not instantly recognisable. There was no drug addicts as such.*

---

# The Old World Club
## 11 STONEGATE, YORK.

# OPENING NIGHT
## WEDNESDAY, OCTOBER 11th.
### YORK'S NEW NIGHT-SPOT WITH FULL CLUB FACILITIES

THE PLACE TO WINE, DINE AND DANCE IN A FRIENDLY OLDEN TIME ATMOSPHERE OF SERVING WENCHES, MINSTRELS AND CABARET — BE IT WITH YOUR WIFE/MOTHER/SISTER/GIRL-FRIEND/BROTHER/FRIEND OR BUSINESS COLLEAGUE.

OPEN NIGHTLY (EX. MONDAYS) 8 p.m. to 12 MIDNIGHT

MEMBERSHIP NOW OPEN — APPLY BY LETTER:—
## The Secretary 11 Stonegate.

---

*The Old World Club and the British School of Motoring, Stonegate, 1970s (Martin Boyd)*

*The 1900th celebrations were in 1971. The Festival club was in the De Grey Rooms and a lot of people would spill into Stonegate. They also used to do Mystery Plays on the back of wagons at the top of Stonegate. I remember one Christmas day and it had been snowing and we found ourselves at the top of Stonegate and it was all virgin snow right down towards the Minster. Nobody had walked the streets and it looked absolutely fantastic.*

Once Ian became a policeman, he still found the locals very friendly.

*There wasn't much crime in that area. Nothing that made headlines. The police used to lock the bar walls. There was once a chap, one of the local vagrants, and he was charging people to go on the bar walls.*

*Bettys was always the best coffee of course, but they'd give us a coffee so we didn't chase away the customers who parked outside. And I*

Carole Spreadbury was often at the Coffee House.

*Me and Ivor* [later her husband] *did our courting at the Coffee House. He'd lean his bike up against Kilvington's. I was 15, he was 17. We actually met on the dodgems at St George's Field. We'd go in the Coffee House in duffel coats never knowing it would become Mulberry Hall and I'd work there later. In 1959 it was full of life and people coming in. Neal Guppy was there trying to get people to go to the St John's dances. He was always in the coffee shop. It had big bay windows and you could get frothy coffee for 9d.*

*Scorpions at Clifton Hospital, 1964: Phil Calvert on drums* (Mike Colley)

Phil Calvert also recalls the Coffee House, and the restaurant it later became, the Stonegate Grill.

*Nobody had any money, you'd all be in there trying to eke the money out so you could stay there all afternoon. There was a big handsome chap had the place, Nicky Kay. All the girls used to fancy him. The girls who worked behind the bar would come and chat with us and he didn't like that, he'd throw us out and we'd give him some awful lip. Reputedly he'd been in the special forces and he looked a real fit chap. Years later, it was my 21st and my dad was in the police force and he had apparently given Nicky Kay a lot of assistance to open the business. Nicky Kay wanted to show his appreciation and he'd always said, "Bring your family", so my dad said, "We're going for your 21st to Stonegate Grill". I got this lump in my throat, thought he'd remember me. We were treated really well, he put all the best fare on. My dad said, "You probably know my son". He gave me a sidelong glance, "Yes I know him but he seems a good guy now". My old gran was with us too, and it nearly gave her a heart attack, she'd never seen crêpes suzette prepared before, and they brought it to the side of the table, flames going up in a roar, it was quite a classy thing to happen in those days.*

*It was probably the worst closure in York for us. Something went there because it was part of the scene for young people. There was nothing fancy about Little Stonegate then, it was a mucky old street. But the Coffee House was a great place, there'd be people standing all over and outside.*

## Restaurants

One of the first Chinese restaurants in York was the Hong Kong at 34 Stonegate. This had taken over from the Devonshire Tea Rooms.

Ian Gillis remembers

*Phil was playing in a band called the Scorpions when we went in there. The singer was a lad called Stuart Harrison. He would pay 1/9d for curried egg and chips. Phil worked at Shepherd's, he used to pay 2s for either curried beef or chicken and chips. I was earning the most money and I'd have curried prawn, that was 2/6d.*

Phil Calvert was

*in the Hong Kong one night, with Gilly, [Ian Gillis] and Stu Harrison. Geoff, who was a photographer, used to turn up at dances and take photos and he joined us. Some roughnecks were at this table and I don't know what had gone on but this guy stubbed out his cigar in Geoff's dinner. Then suddenly there was a big fracas, tables over and the lot, and the little Chinese bloke on the phone to the police. Gilly grabbed it and said, "It's Officer Gillis here, everything's under control".*

Little Stonegate and Swinegate are now full of bistros and smart restaurants. Oscar's wine bar bistro which had been in Little Stonegate since 1987, moved in November 2008 round the corner to occupy part of what was once the Elim Church, next door to the Biltmore Grill restaurant which opened in 2006. The owner of Oscar's and the Biltmore, Andrew Dunn, had to fight in the courts to take the name of Oscar's with him to the new premises. The Little Stonegate restaurant which was Oscar's is now Stonegate Yard Bar and Brasserie.

David Harrison recalls,

*One of the most interesting events in my time was the setting up of Widd's wine bar in Grape Lane which is now called Wilde's, by Major Geoffrey Widdows and his very lively wife Angela. It only stayed open till about nine at night but it became a very lively place. Angela sang in the Minster choir. She christened me 'Badger' because my house was like badger's house in Wind in the Willows. You'd get members of aristocratic families coming and drinking with people from the market. It was one of 'the' places and one of my places. Angela died rather suddenly and we were rather hurt by it, an enormous number of people came to her funeral.*

*Wilde's, formerly Widd's Wine Bar, and No 19 restaurant in Grape Lane, 2009 (Lesley Collett)*

*Opposite was No 19 Restaurant which has changed hands quite a bit. It was almost my dining room for a time. I also used the one in Grape Lane, and once had a meal with Richard Whiteley of all people. He happened to come in there and we had quite a long chat. And I got to know Oliver Worsley, he had the Grape Lane Gallery, and we went to cricket matches together.*

## Chapter 10

# The Artists

The Stonegate area has a history of art and artists. In John Ward Knowles's 1921 manuscript on 'York Artists', he mentions nineteen in the Stonegate area in the 19th century. Today there are very few. There are no galleries in Stonegate itself, although the Braithwaite Gallery is just round the corner in Low Petergate, and York Antiques Centre and Cavendish Antiques both sell the work of local artists.

In the 1790s, Frederick Ashton had a studio in Minster Gates and is listed as a silk mercer and artist, as well as being an excellent engraver, especially of portraits. In the same period, W J Staveley was a carver and gilder in the street. Mr S Hewson advertised in 1790 that he painted miniatures and portraits. He held a viewing at Mrs Cochrane's in Stonegate. In the 1830s, Mr J Dawson was an engraver, publishing 38 engravings of churches in the city. John Thackray had a studio at 10 Stonegate, and produced many portraits of local people. Kirlew, initially a painter and decorator, used a large room in Stonegate which later became Arthur Cowper's dancing academy. Knowles states it was 'beautifully painted all round its walls with American scenery executed in Tempura'. Samuel Walker started off as a house painter in Grape Lane in the 1820s, moved to Coffee Yard and later to Stonegate, advertising,

*Patent Photographic Portraits taken in a few seconds*
*By the action of light at the Daguerrotype Portrait Gallery,*
*50 Stonegate*
*Portraits in oil and oil paintings cleaned, repaired and backlined.*

His business was taken over by Frank Moore. Mr Evans, a picture framer at 43 Stonegate, framed the water colours painted by Mary Ellen Best, who practised in York in 1830. His premises were advertised as a 'repository of the arts and looking-glass warehouse'. John Sutcliffe, animal painter and lithographic artist, had a studio at number 7 Stonegate in 1848 before moving to London. Henry Smith, a printer at the same premises in the 1860s, produced a fine series of churches of York, painted by William Bevan. A number of lithographers stayed in the area as they painted or engraved pictures of the Minster, which is the most drawn and photographed place in York.

At the turn of the 20th century, number 29 Stonegate was the studio of Thomas Guy, who had been a glass gilder. He gave lessons in oil and water colour painting and was also an Artists' Colourman. Many of his paintings were made into postcards. At number 39 was the carver and gilder Elizabeth Hunsworth, who was helped by her son Wilfred. Henry Roebuck was also a carver and gilder, living at 5 Stonegate. Of his five children, two became French polishers.

There were few women practising as artists, but Celia Davis took over the Moores' studio at 50 Stonegate where she painted and gave lessons in sketching and painting in the 1880s. Constance Anderson, daughter of Dr William Anderson and sister of Dr Tempest Anderson in Stonegate, exhibited in Fine Art exhibitions and took some lessons at York Art School in the same period. In 1901 the Misses Jane and Mary Middleton, who were artists, lived at 7 Stonegate. Alice Knowles, daughter of John Ward Knowles, was also a painter and was elected a member of the Royal Water Colour Society in 1926.

In the second half of the 20th century in York, the term 'artist' is synonymous with the name of the York Four, a group of three painters, John Langton, Russell Platt, Reg Williams and one potter, David Lloyd-Jones. John Langton is referred to as 'the north's senior painter'. He was born in the city in 1932, trained at York School of Art and later the Art School in Guildford. He exhibited his first work in 1953 in Leeds Art Gallery, his first solo exhibition in the Austin Hayes Gallery in York in 1961, and since then he has had well over 100 shows, including

*Gill Douglas in her studio (Gill Douglas)*

*of work in it. But it was the first time I put my prints out, it was half prints and half paintings. I was able to get all the prints I've developed over the past four years, because I had my new printing press, I could get the colours and the balance and the right paper.*

231

Many of Gill's paintings are inspired by the sea, including one of a lighthouse keeper's cottage on Little Ross Island which is off Kirkcudbright.

> *My house is called the 'Lighthouse', and it's got 57 stairs from top to bottom. Five different levels and one room on each floor.*

*Staircase of Gill's house, 'The Lighthouse', in Petergate.* (Gill Douglas)

She was exhibiting at the Treasurer's House and met a couple there,

> *and they said, "We're interested because we don't exactly own a lighthouse but we have a little lighthouse keeper's cottage on Little Ross Island. It's a fantastic place, only half a mile long and all there is,*

*Mr Barker probably advised you what to buy, but I read books and I'd go to him and say, "Well have you got this colour or that colour?", or, "I like that kind of watercolour paper, can you get some?". It was only a small place, they had a room downstairs where they kept all the art materials, but they did picture framing upstairs, and they used to act as agents. When the York Art Society had exhibitions you could take your pictures to Barker's and he would send them all in. The Art Society would run exhibitions in the Art Gallery once a year and in the City Library. One or two members came from Scarborough and Bridlington and outlying districts. It was a good society. I was a member for about 20 odd years.*

*In those days they called you Sunday painters. There was a little sketching group at Rowntree's, I was a founder member in about 1952. I did demonstrations on painting later on. At Rowntree's William Dealtry ran an art class and he persuaded me to go and join him. So that's how I started. I also belonged to the Constable Art Club, and they were a postal society. You sent your work away to the secretary, and she criticised your work and parcelled them all up, and they were sent round the country in a portfolio. You got about 40 pictures to look at and you could criticise each other's work, it was really interesting.*

*I met all sorts of people. I never went to Art School, I got most of my tuition from the Constable Art Club. I went on one or two painting holidays in Cornwall, and down in Sussex. It was great, and a new life for me actually. I did watercolours mainly. About the only oil I've done was from a watercolour of Aberaeron in Wales. I've been painting in all sorts of places but I like painting round the Scarborough area. You can go and sit on the fish bay and paint on a Sunday afternoon, never see a soul, but you can hear the crowd going by.*

*I came across one or two people who knew each other, who went into Barker's. I've been to Hovingham Hall a couple of times, with the society and we met the Worsley family. He was a friendly man was*

*Sir William. And we went as a group to Swinton Park. The Earl of Swinton lived at Masham, he was a real friendly man. We had a drink of sherry and talked away. "The place is yours, go round".*

*We went to Coxwold once, to Newburgh Priory once. There was one or two good doctors who were painters in York. Judi Dench's father was a painter, old Dr Dench. He was a member of the Art Society. Somebody introduced me to him. We'd each done a painting of a place called Old Bosham in Sussex and we chatted and then the year afterwards I met him again and he didn't recognise my name, so I said to him, "Dr Dench, do you remember Old Bosham?" He said "Oh yes, I remember you now".*

John Addy remembers Stonegate Fine Arts.

*It was a smallish shop. They had some established artists. They were there for about 15 to 20 years. [From the late 1950s to the mid 1970s at number 8]. I did quite a few paintings of the Yorkshire Dales. I took one in and I was surprised when they accepted it. I managed to sell one of Kettlewell, to a woman from Kettlewell so I was quite pleased. I'd taken it from a line drawing. And now 40 years later, I'm back in Stonegate, at the Antiques Centre, I've got a wall of paintings there.*

*I just liked painting from being at school. I like oils 'cos you can put oils right, you can't put watercolours right. But now I do seascapes. I like the movement of waves and sea more than anything.*

Mark Braithwaite was born in York in 1970.

*I decided my university course wasn't quite what it was supposed to be. So I tried to make a living as an artist and I started being a pavement artist outside the Minster. I did that for four years to raise money to get my prints of York done and went from there. I used to drag it out 'cos you weren't allowed to actually do it on the pavement 'cos it's York stone and it stains. If you do traditional pastels on the pavements of York, it will stay there for months. The council made us do them on canvas and remove them every day so it was a work in progress. It would take between two weeks and three months. They were five foot by eight foot, that's quite big. I used to copy some of the old masters. I did some Raphael and Botticelli then I moved to more modern ones. I did some Impressionists, a lot of Monets.*

*There was a lot more tourism back then. I think people had not seen pavement artists in this country as much as in Italy and France. York regulated it and it became a little bit unworkable because of the administration involved and permissions that you had to get. And so you don't really see people doing it now. It's quite unforgiving because it's cold and you get joint problems. I was glad to stop doing it but I quite miss some summer days up at the Minster.*

*I started working in Petergate, got a stall in the street. I've cut that down 'cos I've got a gallery and I'm getting a bit older. Can't stay outside forever, it's too cold especially in winter. Alan Stuttle used to stand outside in Petergate and he retired three or four years ago. I think when Alan started it was a case of you bunged your easel up, now you have to have public liability insurance.*

Mark stored his materials in nearby Mad Alice Lane.

*I had a friend whose father is quite a famous artist, Robert Lankowitz, his son Wolf used to be a pavement artist as well. He opened a gallery, he wanted his house converted which was a derelict building, a great big warehouse and he used it for a studio. He made living accommodation above and renovated it himself. Put a balcony in and everything. We'd wheel our things down into a basement, it was like a lowered floor, four feet down. So you'd have dropped straight down if you wheeled a trolley in.*

*I got my first prints done, originally from Victorian scenes. I researched the streets, found old photographs and created street scenes based on that. I did Petergate and Lop Lane in Duncombe Place, and Stonegate. And then I did one based in the 1920s as a successor to that. It was a bit fuzzy and a naïve style of painting when I first started but got a bit more detailed as I went on. I was quite interested in doing olde worlde type of pictures at the time. I've done about 70 pictures of York and Yorkshire area.*

*I'll do a series of pictures of maybe landscapes and then move on to some figures, like dancers, just to keep interested really.*

Mark and his wife now own the Braithwaite Gallery in Low Petergate.

*We did have a smaller gallery in Stonegate as well inside the Antiques Centre on the second floor. We were there for two or three years. But it was a difficult location for people to get to, they had to climb stairs to get in the gallery. When the café opened, people queued on the stairs and no-one could get past. It was not practical.*

*We came here about six years ago. It used to be Artefacts. I think they had it for about six years. We moved in within two or three months and we had to get the place renovated again because the roof was in. There's one further down, York Fine Arts, they've been there eight or nine years. But galleries have come and gone quite frequently. There was one in Stonegate at the top which used to back onto one in Grape Lane. And another one which used to sell prints underneath, I remember going in there as a teenager.*

*We're actually changing the building, to open a room upstairs. We'll make that a bit select, less pictures on the walls, just originals. And we're becoming a franchise for Jack Vettriano. He's the best selling artist in the country at the moment, and they're dividing it up into areas. We're going to be selling his limited edition prints, we'll be the*

240

*The Braithwaite Gallery, Low Petergate* (Van Wilson)

*only ones in Yorkshire. And we might open it up for exhibitions as well, and hopefully get some new artists to come along. There are other artists here, I don't like it to just rely on my work. We try to employ people interested in art and we have seven employees at the moment.*

*Outside is quite interesting, we've got a courtyard which backs onto the school. Underneath there's the early remains of a Roman fort and they dug it up and had a look a few years ago. It goes under the flags and you can see where they've bricked off an old passage.*

*I like to do figurative work but unfortunately you've got to make a living. The landscape is what people want, but I'd love to be able to do figurative work all the time and portraits. I've just done a series of portraits for Ampleforth School, 14 portraits of the first girls to go through the school. And I'm a regimental artist as well. The Signals Regiment in York, I've done pictures for them. And the 12th Royal Artillery Regiment in Germany. The picture was so big they had to come and get it so they took us over too. We went over for a week to Germany.*

*Now I've got a studio in my house. I used to paint upstairs at the gallery, but I needed more light. It's not necessarily natural light, you have to use different types of wall to get the effect of different lights. You've got to protect your eyes. If you're looking at a white surface and the light's reflecting off it, you can get snow blindness.*

*I am about to have an exhibition in the Living Room of figurative prints. I had one in Newby Hall last year, they invited me to produce a series of figurative drawings and paintings.* [This was exhibited in the hall in a one man show in early 2008]. *We had one of the models with us and she loved it 'cos she got to dress in a great big gown and look like it was from the 1800s and she got to hold all these mirrors and hairbrushes from the period. It was great. Because you live in a place, you don't realise how lucky you are. It's all there for you in York. It's very pretty, and you've got the bells ringing and you can go round the Minster area, it's quite light and sunny. We're very spoilt.*

## *Hannon's*

One of the best known Stonegate businesses at number 1 Stonegate was, for over 20 years, Hannon's greengrocer's, largely selling rare and exotic fruit. The building was owned by Banks music shop from 1868 to 1918. George Bernard Hannon bought the property in 1948 at a cost of £2250, which was repaid by 1954. The building had been a temporary post office in 1945-46.

The Hannon shops actually started in York in 1880. George's father Martin Hannon had come over from Cork in Ireland and married Katherine, who lived in Portland Street. They had nine children. Martin built up a chain of florists and fruiterers, and eventually had five shops. He moved to St Helen's Square after the First World War, when the street was widened. The label on his bags read,

> M. Hannon
> Fruiterer and Florist
> 34 Gillygate, St Helen's Square
> 28 Blossom Street, 73 Bootham
> National telephone 380
> Strawberries fresh daily

His four sons all went into the business, Billy had a market stall, Alf ran the Bootham shop, George ran Gillygate and St Helen's Square and the other son Peter probably ran the Blossom Street shop. The shop at 2 Micklegate opened in 1928 and remained there for 30 years. Another shop had opened in Stonegate and George ran this. His son John Anthony Hannon was born in 1931, went to St Peter's School, then did National Service. He returned to work at the Stonegate premises with his brother Peter Bland Hannon. Martin died in 1954 at the age of 98. In 1957 John had married Sheila (from Scarborough) and they had five children. In 1963, George retired and John and Peter became the company directors. Sheila worked part-time in the shop when the children were older, in the mid 1970s. George died at the age of 80 in 1969 and Peter died in 1971, leaving John in sole charge.

The shop was unusual because it specialised in fruit which could not be bought anywhere else at that time. John went each morning to buy fruit and vegetables from the big wholesale market in the centre of Leeds. He would get up at 4.30am and was out by 5am, then came back to open up the shop. John knew his fruit, and he was known for quality rather than quantity. He would feel the fruit and inspect the boxes and trays carefully before purchasing. But when he sold the fruit he would be insulted if customers felt it, because he thought they should be able to check it by sight and smell.

The customers were initially local, but then restaurants would come to buy fruit, and later supermarkets. One man came from a restaurant on the North Yorkshire Moors, and later when he moved to Scarborough, still came once a week. Regulars often became friends, but as time went on, there were more tourists than locals. They sold a lot of different vegetables, including celeriac, aubergines, asparagus, carrots, salad vegetables, and mange tout from Morocco. They obtained raspberries from a grower in Scotland who put them on the train overnight. Fruit was fresh daily apart from oranges, apples and bananas and was never frozen. In 1981, their list of fruit included –
Grapefruit from Cuba, pink grapefruit, plums and cranberries from the USA, lemons and limes from Florida, green and purple grapes, oranges and satsumas from Spain, yellow honeydew melons and Gallian melons from Israel, tomatoes from Guernsey and Spain, Bramley's and Cox's apples, Granny Smith's and Red Delicious from France, cherries from South Africa, bananas from the Windward Islands, kumquats, star fruit, ugli fruit, custard apples, coconuts, passion fruit and Tamarillos (a red oval fruit also called tree tomato, but not sweet) from Kenya, Sharons (also known as kaki) and dates from Israel, a lot of nuts including chestnuts from Italy, Colmas from Belgium (special hot house grapes which were quite expensive), pineapples from Ivory Coast, pawpaw

the landing is a hidey-hole, painted blue, now behind a glass cabinet, with a possible secret passage. The two rooms on the first floor are offices, with a workshop for restoration and repairs, mainly of jewellery. Another man restores porcelain. The shop rents out sections to different people, who display their goods in cabinets. John Addy, mentioned in the chapter on artists, has a section selling books on art and an alcove of his pictures.

In the past only the ground floor was the shop, with flats upstairs, and a basement. The small garden at the back is shared with Little Bettys, and is quite a sun trap, with trees, and bird feeders, and a view of St Wilfred's tower and the Minster on the right. Jenny Hall has worked there for eight years.

*There are supposed to be two lots of ghosts, a gentleman whose wife fell and broke her neck on the attic stairs so he hung himself in the attic. There were children who lived in there. Their father died and his wife was scared to come down in case she got attacked. So she and the children starved to death. Lots of people say they have a strange feeling in the jeweller's bit on the second floor. A medium said there was a lady ghost with a huge diamond.*

## British School of Motoring

Although it was not a family business, the British School of Motoring at number 12 Stonegate was well-known (see p. 204). David Poole learnt there in

*1962 or 1963, in a Wolseley 1500. They were a rather classy small car of the time. The BSM used to run quite a few of them, their standard car for learners. We started our lesson from Stonegate. The instructor took you right into Petergate and then wended his way up Stockton Lane.*

*There weren't as many driving schools as there are now. I started off in the April, took my test in June, failed it but passed about the end of July. I didn't have a car and my only experience was the lesson once a week. I think I had 10 hours. Then I bought a small car, and I was able to get one or two external lessons. I was taught by a real dapper little fella called Ray Rathmell. He died young, he was a good instructor. No matter where you went in York for your lesson, he always seemed to know loads of women who he used to wave to.*

*I had most of my lessons on a lunchtime, 'cos working at St Leonard's I just popped out for an hour. You could pay extra if you wanted Sunday mornings, it was five shillings an hour more than the standard weekday hourly rate, which was something like 15 shillings. I would only be earning no more than £700 a year. Petrol was just under five shillings a gallon and car tax probably £12. In those days you could easily park for five minutes between lessons without causing any obstruction. I don't know whether the chaps would take them home on an evening. I know that they had some flexibility 'cos once my usual car was out of action for some reason and the instructor had been and brought a car down from one of the Teesside branches. Same model but a different car. I suppose they would leave there when it became a foot street.*

Ian Gillis recalls,

*When I was at tech college, the British School of Motoring had their shop in Stonegate. At that time you could park down one side. For my 17th birthday I was bought a set of driving lessons. I turned up and they sat me behind this Vauxhall Victor car and I had to manoeuvre it out of the parking site and down Petergate and out into the suburbs. And that's my one abiding memory of Stonegate as a sort of semi adult. It's not the widest of roads and having never driven a car before, to do that, I think the driving instructor was taking his life in his hands.*

## *Walker's*

Roy and Tony Walker were born in York in 1934 and 1938. Their grandfather Edgar George Walker was born in 1874 and owned a house and business in Little Stonegate, built by his grandfather Joseph, who set up the building firm in 1848. It is now the restaurant La Tapas. The brothers would often visit, as Roy explains,

*There were many Walkers, it started off with Joseph, he was born in 1813. He was a builder. His son was George* [one of eleven children] *and his grandson Edgar George. George Alexander was our father and Martha Anne Walker, that's mother. She lived to be nearly 90. We went to Grandad's usually on Christmas Day. He had a gate at the side, Walker's Passage and it went through to Davygate. There was a chap called Bullivant at the other side of the fence, he had two horses. That became the Gas Board and they kept their vans in there right up to Myers and Burnell's. Brown's entrance is there now. you'd get cars coming in and out at the same time. It was a beautiful building. There were at least four rooms upstairs in the attic.*

*I knew Ben Kilvington, he played cricket the same time as I did. He had the shop on the corner which is now Mulberry Hall. I*

*York Gas Company offices, Davygate*
(*York Oral History Society*)

261

*Roy and Tony Walker, 1940* (Roy Walker)

*once looked in, there must have been 10 or 15 chaps working there.
Next door to him was Theakston's plumbers and Ray Theakston was
the son, about my age. One of the lads in the same class as me at
school lived at the pub* [the Coach and Horses in Swinegate]. *It was
a massive building. We had a good party there, a whale of a time. In
Little Stonegate, there was Kilvington's and what had been a chapel,
then in between were four or five houses. I remember the youngsters
all sat on the steps at the front door. But it's all changed, it's been
rebuilt. The other chapel is still there with its original brickwork
and entrances* [Ebenezer Chapel, now Border's], *it was a printer's
underneath. You could walk along and look down and see them doing
the printing.*

*Tony and I finished up being electricians not builders. I went in the
forces and then to the Electricity Board and worked there till I retired.
It was down where Radio York is.*

*Father was secretary to the Building Industry for Yorkshire. He finished up being president. He died in 1949 [aged 49]. And I think it was such a shock, Grandad died within six weeks. That ended the house and everything else.*

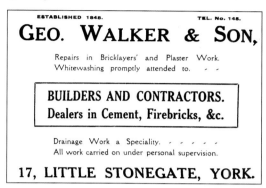

Tony Walker recalls their father,

*We were only young when father died and we didn't see a lot of him. He would chase about delivering and after the evening meal, the dining room table was opened out and he had plans and he was estimating. Night after night after night.*

*As a hobby, he used to race motorcycles on Knavesmire Road, speed trials, 28 mile an hour. So the house on Shipton Road was called Brooklands. In his spare time, before they were married, he worked for grandfather but he was so poorly paid that he used to be projectionist at what turned out to be the Tower Cinema. Walker's built all the houses down that part of Shipton Road. The one we had cost about £450 to build. Mother and father got that as a wedding present in 1930.*

*They were business travellers, that's the origin of the name Walker. If you went back in history to 1066 or something, they've always been in York. At the end of the war, any work over £10, they had to get special government permits to do the work. I remember once he'd been on a*

*George Walker, Grand Vizier, St Saviourgate Masonic Lodge* (Roy Walker)

*farm and he had a dozen eggs which was unheard of during the war. Mother took half a dozen up the road to the Managing Director of Rowntree's, 'cos he lived on Shipton Road.*

*When we went for Christmas to Little Stonegate, and it was the King's speech, we all had to stand to attention and say nothing, then, 'God save the King'. It was very Victorian. Children were seen and not heard. I remember saying, "Don't you mean heard and not seen?" And I picked myself up off the floor. That was the way you were brought up in those days. Granddad was part of the Masonic Lodge and he was The Grand Vizier. Boyes from Boyes and Harding's from High Ousegate, they set up this lodge, members of the Gentlemen's Club where the pizza parlour is now* [on Lendal Bridge]. *Also there* [in Little Stonegate] *in the '50s, York City Supporters' Club had a building. I used to play football for Cliftonville and they were the junior club for York City Football Club. We'd go upstairs for meetings, and they'd put road safety films on there for school-kids. That was in Myers and Burnell's garage entranceway.*

*When we were kids, if we were in town, we always went there, used to finish up with sixpence for ice-cream. Then opposite the end of Little Stonegate we went upstairs and it was a gents' hairdressers. It was*

street, it was full of crowds. John went out to see her and for some reason he was crying, and the Princess stopped and said, 'Don't cry'.

Both Mr and Mrs Richardson say they were very happy there and were sad when the business closed. They had made a lot of friends, and many would go through into the bakery to see the couple. Although the business did well locally, Michael said they never made any money. It was also very tying and they had one week's holiday a year. Michael started work at 5am and would work until two or three o'clock. Having a social life was difficult.  Their busiest times were Christmas and Easter.  They made lots of Christmas cakes, mince pies and brandy snaps in winter. At Easter they made Simnel cakes, and a great many hot cross buns, as well as Easter eggs. Michael bought the chocolate and poured it into Easter egg moulds then decorated them. He also made wedding cakes. John helped out in the shop as a child. He recalls that later on when he went out to work, on Friday nights near Easter and Christmas he would help his father in the bakery until the early hours. They opened Saturdays but closed Wednesday afternoons as did most York shops in those days. When the policemen did their early rounds, the local one would always come in for a cup of tea.

In the 1960s they opened a café on the first floor. The staff included Mrs Lee and Michael's Aunt Molly. They served hot meals and it was popular but they closed it in about 1970. At that period things began to slow down as supermarkets opened up, and they finally sold the shop in 1980, as Michael and Dorothy neared retirement age. But Michael still does baking for people from home although he is now nearly 83. He won a national award in September 1977 for 'work on behalf of the deaf in York'.

The printer's devil which exists on the corner of Coffee Yard, just outside the bakery, belonged to the Greenwoods. It had been languishing in the cellar for some time and then in 1951 for the Festival of Britain, Michael had it painted red rather than the black it had been before. In 1975 the horns were broken by vandals who lassoed it, and Michael repaired it. His great friend Martin Dutton, the wood carver, who once worked for Dick Reid and did the carving for Fairfax House, made the couple a replica of the printer's devil out of wood, with a pen pot at the back. Dutton once worked for Thompson's of Kilburn, and rather than the Thompson's mouse, his trademark is a lizard.

Michael's father George Royden was one of six brothers and the family had a printing firm Wood & Richardson in King's Square, which had been founded by Thomas Wood. He was director from its formation in 1905 until his retirement in early 1939 and died aged 67 in December 1939. He had been secretary of St Michael le Belfrey Cricket Club and treasurer of York Tradesmen's Angling Association.

*George Royden Richardson at munitions factory in the Second World War.*

(Michael Richardson)

George Royden was also a sporting man and was appointed president of the English Bowling Association in 1963. He died in September 1969 aged 72. He had also been a freemason, based at the lodge in St Saviourgate. His younger brother Noel Richardson ran the printers during the war, as George managed a munitions company. There was a disagreement and Noel went into business on his own taking over

Coultas and Vollans printers in Little Stonegate. This then became Noel Richardson & Co. in 1958. John Richardson followed his grandfather into the Wood & Richardson printer's and was managing director by the time he had reached his thirties. After more than 80 years in business, the company moved out of King's Square because of proposed traffic bans and bought the former Co-op Dairy on Haxby Road in November 1986. (See Chapter 4, Booksellers and Printers).

George Royden's youngest brother, Linden Richardson, was a pilot in the First World War, and was killed in an air accident at the age of 19 in April 1918. He kept a diary for the period December 1917 to the day before his death, which is to be published. Noel's son, also called Linden Richardson, took over as director of Noel Richardson's in Little Stonegate in 1975.

Kathy Parker, who worked at Jackson's Signs, recalls

> *The most magical place of all was Richardson's Bakery. I've never had bread like that ever. We used to have cheese bread cakes warm out of the oven.*

## York Medical and Surgical Company

John and Myra Atkinson ran this business at 18 Stonegate in the 1950s, but moved in 1969 and transferred the shop to Colliergate, operating as M and J Surgical Stores. Their daughter Kate Atkinson, a well-known author, who was born in 1951, won the Whitbread Prize in 1995 for her first novel, *'Behind the Scenes at the Museum'*. Part of the book is set in Stonegate, where the central character Ruby Lennox lives with her family in what is referred to as 'The Shop', a pet store not unlike what was part of Kilvington's. Kate uses her knowledge of the city to set the scene. At one point her character walks up Stonegate and visits Richardson the baker's for a 'large floury white loaf',

*Ebor Prep. School Harvest Festival, 1960s*
*Van Wilson at right, Kate Atkinson second from right at back.* (Van Wilson)

and then Hannon's 'for apples, spring cabbage and potatoes'. After a fire in the premises, Ruby's father George decides to go in for a new line of business, 'Medical and Surgical Supplies'. He gets very enthusiastic about it, 'Trusses, wheelchairs, hearing aids, elastic stockings, walking sticks, there's no end to it'. There follows a very amusing scene with Ruby let loose amongst the surgical supplies, pretending to be a Dalek in an electric wheelchair, using 'a dismembered dummy leg that models an Elastanet two way stretch stocking, with two miniature bakelite torsos, who face each other, displaying their little surgical corsets'. (Adrian Gell talks about the practical jokes carried out by staff there and at Inglis's in the chapter on Craftsmen).

## W P Brown

The company was started as a linen draper's in Nessgate in 1891 by
Alderman Henry Rhodes Brown, who was 26 at that time. He had
three children, Lily, William Percy and Henry Rhodes Brown junior, who all joined the firm. There was a warehouse in Swinegate.
Then the shop, selling soft furnishings and fancy goods, moved to
Davygate. In March 1900, the 'Grand Opening of the Emporium'
took place. The family also had at that time a 'Sixpence Halfpenny
Bazaar' and a 'Penny Bazaar and Domestic Stores' in Church Street.
Alderman Brown had been a Blue Coat School boy and had risen
through his hard work and determination to run the business, and
become Lord Mayor twice, in 1913 and 1932. William Percy Brown
managed the shop but died at the age of 38 in 1930, and his brother
Henry Rhodes junior ran the business from 1929 until 1982. It is
probably the only shop in the city to be run by five generations of
one family.

*Brown's Store, Davygate Corner*  (Paul Stabler)

William's daughter, Margaret (Peggy) Goldie, nee Brown, recalls,

*I was born in Poppleton in 1919, when my father came back from the war, because it was a forerunner of nursing homes. We lived over the shop, and to get upstairs you had to come through the shop, and my parents didn't think it was suitable. My parents weren't stern, they were quite lenient. I think we were Daddy's girls, he used to take us out and make a fuss of us. He died when I was ten, so we missed him a lot.*

*He won a medal for gallantry* [in the First World War]. *He didn't come home immediately because he was wounded, in hospital. We lived at the shop until I was four years old, then we moved out, because the bedrooms were full of stock, to 60 Scarcroft Hill, looking over the Knavesmire, where I lived until I was fourteen. We had eight bedrooms. My sister had a room, my parents had a room, I had a room, a spare bedroom, the maid's bedroom, the playroom, boxroom and my mother's sewing room. Mother was a lady of leisure, my father wouldn't have her in the business, because his own mother was always working and he wanted her to be at home with the children. She socialised, she used to give bridge parties and whist drives. My father's friends often came to the house. We'd start the evening by singing round the piano, or play cards round the big dining table. They drank port wine, and smoked. We were allowed from quite an early age to stay up and take part on a Saturday night. It all stopped when my father died, my mother didn't entertain.*

*At Christmas we all went to my grandfather's* [Henry Rhodes Brown] *at Allerthorpe. We all sat round the big dining table, a turkey at one end, goose at the other.* [On Christmas Eve] *he would come round and knock on our doors and tell us if we didn't go to sleep Father Christmas wouldn't come. We'd get up Christmas morning, go to church, and when we came back, our parents had laid out all the presents, heaps for each person. Dolls' prams, dolls, sometimes useful ones like fur gloves, quite big presents, and once an aeroplane about*

*we got the opportunity to buy that in 1992 and that was the last piece of the jigsaw. If we were having to pay the market rent for this, I don't think we'd be here. We've watched rents in York go up phenomenally. But this recession is going to force rents back down to reasonable levels. We've also got a store in Helmsley that has been open about 11 years and we're opening a third store in Beverley in April 2010.*

*At one stage we used to be more wholesalers but as cars came in, we moved into pure retailing. We have concessions, 60 per cent is ours and 40 per cent other people. They put stock in and staff in and we take a percentage of the sales. You get the specialisms of the people running those companies. Fashion is sourced mainly in the Far East and India and these people have got skills and management teams to be over there doing it, whereas off our own bat we wouldn't be able to. It was very important to York when Coppergate 2 got rejected because it meant that companies like H and M, and Zara made decisions to come in. The more competition, the better it is, 'cos it makes more people visit your city.*

*We started off as drapers, that's still a strong area for us. Haberdashery and wool died a death, but we have linens and we've moved much more into fashion. The biggest area is cosmetics and beauty, and handbags and accessories. Ladies' handbags has seen a phenomenal growth, ladies seem to collect handbags like they collect shoes.*

*When pedestrianisation came, it was a very good move for York, it makes it a much better environment for people to wander round the streets. We've got the beautiful architecture, the pubs, the restaurants, not just the shopping, it all comes together as a mix. We now have the Brown's gold card, about 4200 of those. Originally it was a Brown's Shopping Club and people paid money in and if they didn't spend it, we'd give them interest at the end of the year, but it was an old fashioned system. Now they have the Brown's credit card, buy it first, pay later. That's become the way of the world.*

*We have 147 staff though it fluctuates. We tend to have more 'pay and pack' points so there's more staff and it avoids these lengthy queues. In the olden days, when we opened, there'd be 100, 150 people queuing on a Saturday morning. But things have shifted later and now you don't really get busy in the city centre till half past ten. We've got a lot of staff who've been here ten years or more. In my father's day, many staff would do 30 or 40 years. If you lose somebody, you lose the knowledge that person's collected, you've got to retrain someone.*

*There's some very good retail independents in York. I'm a member of the Merchant Taylors. Communication between us is good, collectively we are better working together. The family has always supported the council in York. The council has been a big success, the way it's maintained buildings in York. Henry Rhodes's philosophy was 'Let's go big in York and try and make bigger trading space'. That's what the company did, obviously that was a pretty good decision. The buildings now are 55,000 square feet right in the middle of York, a grade A site in the city. It's lovely, you've got Stonegate, Petergate, Davygate and all the little lanes, the Quarter area, Grape Lane and Back Swinegate, a lovely shopping environment.*

*We've got a lady, Lisa, who does the window displays. We do a lot with the local community. Cabaret was on at the Opera House so we did a window with some of the cast in it. Jimmy Osmond is coming to York so we're going to have a window with him. They're our big strength, we've got a large amount of window space. We do a lot with hosiery and lingerie, and sometimes our hairdressers do live displays in there, that's been successful.*

*My father worked here for 50 years, Henry Rhodes Junior worked here for 50 years, and Paul Stabler, Margaret Goldie's son, he did 50 years. Quite something. There'll be very few in York with so many generations and I've got a son and he might one day say he wants to be the sixth. I love it here. I've been here 27 years, so I could be destined to do 50. But we're very lucky, it's a beautiful city to work in, lovely people to work with. Hopefully we manage to change with the times, the key thing is spotting the changes in society and making sure you react to that. We have had sales growth in the last few years so we have been bucking the trend a little bit.*

## Greenwood's

William Greenwood was a cabinet maker at 24 Stonegate from the mid 19th century until the 1940s. When Robert Sunter the bookseller owned 23 Stonegate (now 35), he decided he did not need the whole premises and built a brick partition wall in the shop. John Ward Knowles (see chapter on craftsmen) bought the business and leased the old chapel and the partitioned part which was 23a Stonegate, to the Greenwoods. The chapel later deteriorated and by 1963 was so derelict that it had to be demolished.

OLD SWANSEA VASES.

CHIPPENDALE CHAIR.     OLD QUEEN ANNE CABINET     A pair of XVIIth Century Carved Wood Columns.

ESTABLISHED 1829.

THE OLD CURIOSITY SHOP,
where one can purchase beautiful OLD FURNITURE, CHINA, SILVER AND CURIOS at reasonable prices.

**W. F. Greenwood & Sons,**
LTD.
**24, Stonegate, YORK.**

The Greenwoods actually started out in business in 1829, and were in High Ousegate until they moved to Stonegate in March 1849. An advertisement in 1851 described them as 'Cabinet Maker, Upholsterer,

Undertaker, Dealer in new and second hand furniture'. The furniture was moved from their warehouse in Jubbergate to rooms in Chapel Yard, Grape Lane and Coffee Yard. When William Greenwood died, the business was carried on by his widow Jane in 1861. In July 1864 their son William Frances succeeded to the business. In 1886, he was described as 'Dealer in decorated works of art, licensed valuer, cabinet maker and upholsterer'. Mate's Illustrated Guide of York 1906 described Greenwood's as 'the Old Curiosity Shop'. The firm bought other premises in Grape Lane and rented these out, as Gary Greenwood explains.

*In what is now Norman Court in Grape Lane, there was a cork maker above the picture framers. Where the old chapel was, there are now flats. We bought it from Miss Knowles for about £400. When the chapel was demolished, we had to have a dig before the flats were built and an archaeology company at Malton took away bones. Miss Knowles had the cottage at the back of the antique shop, reputedly haunted. Stained glass was still there upstairs. Mr Downs the printer was in the corner unit of Norman Court. And at what is now 1331 Restaurant, there were two units below. Dick Reid was in the bottom part, he was the first tenant of Greenwood's. There was also a staircase at the front leading up to Noel Beech, the picture framer, and Kites restaurant at the top. Ambience sold second hand furniture. We owned the El Piano building, it had to be rebuilt for them. Our business closed down about 1978. The shop called Jigsaw was Greenwood's. My grandfather lived at the top. The floors were all concrete to keep out the rain. The inside has been altered substantially. It became Pitlochry then the Edinburgh Woollen Mill.*

*I worked at the shop from 1960 for thirty years. York then was known as the Sleepy City. There was a photo of my uncle eating sandwiches on the step, with no-one else in the street. In the 1960s the property was a liability, in such bad shape. Birch's did it up, at a cost of £335,000. They used big supports. The outside is now listed.*

*Queen Mary visits Greenwood's with Alfred Augustus Greenwood and chauffeur*
*(Greenwood's)*

Audrey Peace lived in Finkle Street as a child and remembers one of the most famous customers of the shop.

> *I saw Queen Mary twice at the antique shop, Greenwood's. I didn't know who it was. I'd be playing and I went in and told my mother about this posh lady with this big hat and she said, "She's seen t'old mother", and then I came in and said I'd seen her again. Apparently she went quite regular unannounced to Greenwood's. I think the second time I realised who it was. It was just a normal day, during the afternoon. I must have been off school. It didn't get crowded like it does now.*

Outside the present shop is a photo of Queen Mary's visit. The first time she called, the shop was closed, so a girl called Bessie Haggerty, lodging opposite at the Georgian Tea Shop, went to fetch Mr Greenwood. The Prince of Wales, later King Edward VIII, was with his mother, and said to Bessie, "Don't worry about me, you look after Ma". Queen Mary was known as an avid collector of antiques, adding considerably to collections in Royal Households such as Holyrood House in Edinburgh.

## Myers and Burnell

Christopher Myers was a coach builder and harness maker in Little Stonegate, who was initially in business with a man called Brearey, but by 1829 was running it alone. In 1835 he was appointed as coach-maker to HRH Princess Victoria and HRH the Duchess of Kent. He died in 1832 and his widow Ann Myers continued until 1836 when she took her son in law Mr Burnell into partnership. The Burnells were already in the same business. James Burnell had been a coachmaker in Davygate, advertising as far back as 1783. He had been apprentice and foreman for his uncle Martin Burnell, who opened the Davygate premises in 1781 in the place which had been occupied by Cochran and Cartwright, and eventually became a partner. In 1801 they were advertising for the return of a runaway apprentice. The partnership was dissolved in 1802 and he continued alone. In June 1837 the newly formed Myers and Burnell patented their new coach. In 1843, tragedy struck when a coachmaker was killed by falling wheels, and a few

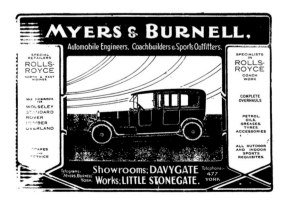

*1923*

years later, in September 1849, there was a fire at the premises, necessitating a move to 17 Little Stonegate in December. Ann Myers died in 1858 but the firm kept its name and business flourished. In 1885 they were engaged as coachbuilders, harness makers and heraldry painters to the High Sheriff of Yorkshire.

David Poole remembers them.

*1960s*

*Quite an old firm in York, they were bespoke coach makers for horse carriages originally. But nobody was wanting coaches built when cars came along, so they started to build bespoke car bodies, buying the mechanical parts and building the body around it. I don't know how they got their expertise or mechanics but that's what they did. The original garage went through from Davygate, the back entrance next to the rear of Brown's department store. They were a big firm, agents for Standard Vanguard Company. I don't think anybody else could sell Standard in York.*

*One of our neighbours worked for Myers and Burnell as a car mechanic well into the '50s. The chap who ran it was called Johnny Kay, he was Lord Mayor about 1948. Grape Lane was quite derelict then, but round the back Bellerby's used to have a garage, they had a Rolls Royce as a works van, it was a Rolls Royce frame and they adapted it, a big box on the back.*

*They must have had quite a workshop behind there because they employed joiners as well as painters and decorators. Bellerby's did a lot of prestigious stuff for country houses, and they'd do ceilings in*

*Castle Howard, things like that. They were good craftsmen. Derek was a good sportsman, he played hockey for England in the early 50s. One of his lads is on Radio York, Jules Bellerby.*

In 1955 Myers and Burnell opened up a new depot in Dunnington and announced in 1965 that they would continue to trade at Dunnington and Stockhill Garage, when they were taken over by Robert B Massey.

## Mulberry Hall

Michael Sinclair was born in Doncaster in April 1942 and,

*arrived in York in January 1962. My mother had a smallish china shop in Doncaster. I went off to work in Wolverhampton for three years with quite a well known store group called James Beatty. My mother in the meantime opened a small branch in Stonegate, and I came up in 1962 to run it for her. After a couple of years they suggested I buy the shop which I did in 1965. My father said, "Go and borrow the money and I'll guarantee the overdraft". So I bought the little bit of medieval property, the original Mulberry Hall bit, about 600 square feet on the ground floor. We checked with one or two historians in York and they said Mulberry could be a derivation of Mowbray, 'cos the Mowbray family had it at one stage. But there was apparently a mulberry tree in the back yard so it could have come from that.* [In medieval times, a mansion called Mowbray Hall or Mulberry Hall, stood between Little Stonegate and Petergate, a connection with the North Yorkshire Mowbray family].

*There was traffic in the street to begin with. The shops were pretty well all private traders, a very happy collection of people. The shops thrived and in a sense complemented each other. I can remember very happy times but lots of problems with getting goods in. Most of them came*

*Mulberry Hall, 2009 (Lesley Collett)*

by rail, and glass and china came in great casks full of straw. We had a very bad tempered railway driver who would ferry the goods from the station depot. Our casks were so heavy and big, he used to throw them off his vehicle in fury. There was a great resounding crash when they hit the floor, but they were so well packed we never had any breakages. Quite often they were so big, we had to unpack them in the street, but other traders were very helpful and would muck in and help us.

*The chap who was the great expert on Stonegate was Ben Kilvington. When I first came, his mother lived over the shop, she used to sit up there and watch the street go backwards and forwards, a wonderful old lady. There was John Hannon, the fruiterer, he told stories about skating on the river and going through the ice. Janet Banks was a strong lady, ran a wonderful business, one of the best things in Stonegate. She was a sort of matriarch. There was Inglis's across the road and I always had a good relationship with Angela of Droopy and Brown, I had respect for her, she ran a good business. Women somehow are good at seeing things that men don't always pick up. There was a lot more spirit about the street then.*

Of the businesses mentioned, only Mulberry Hall and Inglis survive. Many people were surprised when Michael announced he was leaving the business and going to become an Anglican vicar. He went on to be in charge of eight churches in the parish of West Buckrose, based at All Saint's Church, Burythorpe. He officially retired in 2008 but took up a part time post within the Church of England. Adam Sinclair and his sister Victoria now run Mulberry Hall, and Adam is also a trustee of York Civic Trust. Michael explains,

*I started training in '94 and was ordained in 1997. It was always there loitering at the back of my mind but I had a family and a business to run. But I came back to it. I wasn't sad to leave. I've been back but haven't been running the show. They [his son and daughter] run the show. I was very happy that they took it on and they've continued in the same vein. There are staff who have been there for years. That conti- nuity is important, that the staff are cared for and valued. You can have super premises but at the end of the day it's the people. The nature of retail business is that it appeals to women more than it appeals to men, and on the whole the warehouse jobs appeal to men more. We've always had a predominance of women. I think to be in a shop you have to enjoy it. If you're itching for half past five to come round, it's no good.*

*Michael (left) and Adam Sinclair (second from right)* (Michael Sinclair)

Carole Spreadbury worked at Mulberry Hall.

*I started 1982. I worked there for 20 years but not continuously. I left to open a guesthouse in '88 for three years but went back to help in the sales. Queues at Mulberry Hall were ten deep for January sales. It was often snowing, and Michael would be giving out mulled wine and drinks. He was very kind. I started in the Wedgwood Shop next to Hannon's. It was a separate shop. That closed and was incorporated into Mulberry Hall. For sales we sometimes rented properties, like the shop Mulberry [in Swinegate], we used that for a few years. We were known everywhere, hundreds came to the sales. When we moved to Cambridge, I still worked at Mulberry Hall three days a week, I did the window displays. I would get up at 5.30am and come on the train and stay overnight at my mum's. I did this for four years, then we moved back to York. The window displays were massive, like the Forth Bridge. We had 16 showrooms inside. The Dining Warehouse opened, I helped set it up. The Duchess of Gloucester opened the Royal Copen-*

*hagen room, it was a special event. Then there was the French crystal room, Lalique and Baccarat.*

*Michael made the staff feel valued. He was excellent to work for, you felt it was a privilege. Every Tuesday morning was a meeting for staff. If somebody was in charge of a department, he'd send you to factories. I went to Copenhagen twice and did a course in Borlaston, Wedgwood. He'd make sure you knew the product then you sold it better. I went to Sheffield and watched cutlery being made. Some went to see porcelain in Hungary, or to Valencia, for Ladbrough. I went round dealing with everything.*

*Michael Sinclair presents the No. 1 Hereford Cathedral plate by Spode to the Lord Bishop of Hereford, to be later presented to the Queen, 1976. Left to right: Venerable Archdeacon of Ludlow, A H Woodhouse; Lord Bishop of Hereford, the Rt. Rev. John Eastaugh; Michael Sinclair; Group Captain Caswell. (Photo: Brian Hankins) (Michael Sinclair)*

*In 1982, the Doulton Shop had been over the road and just closed. They closed the Wedgwood in 1984. It was Yves Rocher for ages. I was part-time there, I was never full-time. Being on the displays, I started earlier when the cleaners were there, about 7.45am to 4 o'clock. I didn't work Saturdays. The window display was ongoing, with a lot of variety. You put yourself in it, it's very personal. We had an annual Christmas dinner and dance at various places, the Merchant Taylors', Merchant Adventurers' or Middlethorpe Hall. It was a big event.*

As Michael says,

*York has grown and grown and some people say too far. But it has brought wealth here. The face of York has changed dramatically, especially in industry. We were certainly in the right place at the right time. When I came, York was like a market town and it just blossomed and grew and has gone from strength to strength and I have to say in our particular niche, it's been very good.*

The general feeling from those people I interviewed was that Stonegate is not the same as it was. The old crafts and traditions have gone, and technology has taken over. Many people are saddened by this, and pleased that they retired when they did. In a time of recession, things are difficult for a lot of people, although some of the larger family businesses that remain, are still offering the quality of merchandise and service they have become known for. But York is still as beautiful as it was, York people are still as lively and interesting as they always were and I hope that this book reflects that, as it offers such a wide and varied range of 'Stonegate Voices'.

# BIBLIOGRAPHY

ATKINSON, Kate        *Behind the Scenes at the Museum.* Doubleday 1995

KNIGHT, C. B.         *A History of the City of York.* Herald Printing Works 1944

KNOWLES, John Ward    *Stonegate.* Manuscripts 1923

MURRAY, Hugh          *Directory of York Pubs.* Voyager Publications 2004

MORGAN, Peter (ed.)   *Ousebeat Magazine* April 1964

POWELL, J.            *Godfrey of York: A Tale of Bumps and Books.* John Powell 1988

SESSIONS, W. & M.     *Printing in York.* Sessions 1976

SEYMOUR, Brian        *York's Other Churches and Chapels.* Highgate Publications 1992

STACPOOLE, Ed A.      *Noble City of York.* Cerialis Press 1972

WADDINGTON, P.        *Patrick, or That Awful Warning.*
                      Patrick Waddington, Sessions 1986

WILLIS, Ronald        *Nonconformist Chapels of York 1693-1940*
                      York Georgian Society 1964

York Censuses 1861-1901

Kelly's Directory 1872-1973

Stevens Street Directory of York 1881

Yorkshire Evening Press

Yorkshire Gazette

# OTHER BOOKS BY THE SAME AUTHOR

*The History of a Community: Fulford Road District of York.*
University College of Ripon and York St John, 1984

*Alexina: A Woman in Wartime York.* Voyager Publications, 1995

*Rich in All but Money: Life in Hungate 1900-1938.* York Archaeological Trust, 1996
(Revised edition 2007)

*Beyond the Postern Gate: A History of Fishergate and Fulford Road.*
York Archaeological Trust, 1996

*Humour, Heartache and Hope: Life in Walmgate.* York Archaeological Trust, 1996

*York Memories.* Tempus Publishing, 1998

*Number 26: The History of 26 St Saviourgate, York.* Voyager Publications, 1999

*Voices of St Paul's: An Oral History of St Paul's Church* (Edited). William Sessions, 2001

*Rhythm and Romance: An Oral History of Popular Music in York. Volume 1 : The Dance Band Years.* York Oral History Society, 2002

*Something in the Air: An Oral History of Popular Music in York. Volume 2 : The Beat Goes On.* York Oral History Society, 2002

*The Walmgate Story.* Voyager Publications, 2006

*Rations, Raids and Romance: York in the Second World War*
York Archaeological Trust, 2008